DATING STANDARDS THAT SPEAK

10 Dating Habits to Take You From Single to Sought After

JANTAE RASHAUN

Copyright © 2020 by Jantae Rashaun
Published by JTM House Publishers
All rights reserved - It is not legal to reproduce, duplicate, or transmit any part of this document in either electronic means or in printed format. Recording of this publication is strictly prohibited and any storage of this document is not allowed unless with written permission from the publisher except for the use of brief quotations in a book review.
Library of Congress Cataloging-in Publication Data
ISBN: 978-1-7345490-2-7 (paperback)
ISBN: 978-1-7345490-1-0 (ebook)
Printed in the United States of America

CONTENTS

Acknowledgments	v
Introduction	vii
Part One: Get Into Self Work	1
Habit One: Shift Your Mindset	2
Habit Two: Let Your Standards Speak	18
Habit Three: Capture Your Vision	36
Habit Four: Become Your Expectations	44
Habit Five: Curb Your Attractions	55
Habit Six: Check Yourself	75
Part Two: Get Out There	87
Habit Seven: Date with Purpose	88
Habit Eight: Decode His Intentions	95
Habit Nine: Decode His Date	106
Habit Ten: Don't Lose Yourself	121
Final Words	133

ACKNOWLEDGMENTS

I am so grateful for the opportunity to share so many of my love lessons with other women. It makes all of the past tears and moments of heartbreak worth it. I want to acknowledge those who have been by my side during the process of creating this book.

To my husband and two amazing sons, I love you with all my heart. Thank you for loving me, inspiring, and motivating me each and every day. To my best friend and sister, Ki, thanks for always believing in me, lifting me up when I had doubts, and being my unofficial editor -- I love you.

To my Mom and Dad, for raising me to work hard, carry myself with respect, and for being my example of everlasting love. To both of my grandmothers, for the many words of wisdom throughout my life that helped me become the woman I am today. I love you all.

Finally to God, for blessing me with a loving family, gifting me with a passion to help women, and for the chance to walk in my purpose. You are my source.

INTRODUCTION

How many countless hours have you spent discussing with your girlfriends the lack of quality men available on the dating scene? It seems that it's a common occurrence to hear or see, posted on social media, the complaints of women when it comes to the lack of, well, good men in general. You don't see this discussion on the other side of the equation with men, but for some reason you see and hear it with women. If we're not careful, these complaints can grow from seeds of envy to restraints on our lives. "Why does SHE have the perfect relationship? What am I doing wrong? There must be *something* I am doing wrong." Well, maybe there are a plethora of men who just aren't "relationship material." On the other hand, maybe, women can lock themselves into a box where they see success stories and harrowing statistics flung at them like posters that say, "You will never find someone!" The way society functions today -- with social media culture at the forefront -- paints a picture that everyone else seems to be out living their best lives. While you're on an endless dating roller-coaster with all the wrong men, struggling to find love. Stop buying into this message! This thinking is the easiest way to wind up settling for far less than you deserve. The wrong mindset can thrust you into dating habits that actually work against the very thing you're hoping to find: a lasting relationship with the right man.

Every relationship starts with one possibly overused, but oh-so-important word: STANDARDS. You wouldn't believe how many times I have put my heart on the line for the wrong man, and paid for it in the worst way. The truth is, I was a serial monogamist. And for one reason or another, I seemed to constantly invite tumultuous ups and downs, and drastic highs and lows into my love life. Looking back, I realize the common denominator was me. But why? I always believed that I knew my worth and had a clear vision of what I wanted in a man. How did I constantly wind up in relationships that didn't last? I would start out strong, but somehow, the momentum would always seem to shift --

and not in my favor. I came to understand that one of my biggest problems, in addition to overlooked red flags, was that I approached dating with the wrong mindset. I had to overcome so much drama, heartache, and wasted time, because I didn't understand the importance of knowing my standards and sticking to them. Then, it happened! I made a life-changing decision to take note of all of the heart wrenching lessons I'd learned and really put them to use. Not long after, I met an amazing man who proposed to me within *six* months of us dating -- my husband of thirteen years.

What I finally realized along my journey to love was something invaluable that I promised myself I'd never forget. It was this: that standards, paired with the right mindset, are the essential first steps to learning to be intentional about dating. When you allow your standards to speak for you, they lead to habits that make you more desired and pursued by men who are *worthy* of your attention. Standards form habits, and these conscious standards and subconsciously formed habits will lead you to the man who will love you long term. Throughout this book, I will empower you to do the necessary self work to align your standards, change your attractions to the wrong men, and attract a quality man with the best intentions for you.

PART ONE: GET INTO SELF WORK

HABIT ONE: SHIFT YOUR MINDSET

You are the prize and deserve to be pursued.

As women gain equal footing with men in society, there has to be a debate about women's roles in relationships and family. The growing role of women in society has now migrated into the dating and relationship realms. More and more women are ignoring traditional ideas and stepping up to pursue men. As a result, some men have abandoned their instinctive hunting nature and are basking in the fact that they can be chased. Some even expect it. They have begun to buy into this new arrangement as some sort of step towards cultural progress; but in reality, there are a lot of negative aspects attached to the new way. I recently watched a talk show where a well-known relationship coach repeatedly insisted that men should not pursue women. He went even further to say that pursuit of women has a negative impact on the "male ego," as if men are so fragile we should put our pride on the line to preserve theirs. To me, this is ridiculous, and represents so much of what's wrong with the new-age mentality. As cultural and social norms change, you can't completely abandon the way love is defined, or the role men are intended to play in finding it. Giving women the responsibility shifts the natural balance and can lead to long term consequences.

You shouldn't let your newfound strength and power spill over into the dating arena in a negative manner. Yes, take the high-paying leadership position at work. Let the world experience the gifts, talents, and authority that live within you. But don't let men get away with handing women more responsibility in love and relationships. You are the prize they should seek. When you put yourself in the position to initiate, you will have to dictate every step of the relationship as it progresses. The right man will see you as the respectable, beautiful, and precious gift that you truly are. When a man sees your true worth, and wants to love you, he will give himself up for you in pursuit and stop at nothing to win your heart.

Adopting the right mindset for match-making is

the first step to preparing to find the person who will love you according to your standards. Remember that standards and self-worth are the backbone of every habit needed for successful dating. Dating standards that speak for themselves through you are the essence of attracting someone fit to love you. In order to appeal to a man who is ready for something real, you have to be ready yourself. Prepare your mindset for high-standard, clear-purposed dating, and you will find a man who has the same mature, experienced, and equipped mindset.

The most important concept to understand in the search for love is that women deserve to be pursued. You should never feel the need to constantly chase any man. 1 John 4:19 explains this perfectly, *"We love Him because He first loved us."* The right man will *always* pursue you.

Never Pursue A Man

How many times have you been approached by a man who undoubtedly has no chance with you? You politely brush off his advances and go about your day. But why do you think that is? Why do you think this happens to nearly every woman, but not every man? It doesn't matter if a man is super attractive, worth millions, or even in the public eye. Even men that are fully aware they are high on the food chain don't hesitate to pursue women that stand out to them. Standards set you apart; therefore, you actually have a better chance with these men if you exhibit self-control and lead with self worth. If you are confident and hard-to-get, he will continue pursuing, because when you see yourself as a prize, so will he. This same logic applies to every man. He wants to pursue and WILL pursue, but sometimes only for the right woman.

Understand this wholeheartedly: you are worth pursuing. This idea works in tandem with high standards. When you believe that you are a woman worth pursuing, you can "walk in your standards." Then, when you find yourself being actively pursued, your confidence will be elevated, and you will be less likely to accept less than your complete worth. This mindset protects you from falling into unhealthy relationships with men who don't appreciate what you bring to the table. Mindset matters, ladies.

It's important to recognize that the way a romantic encounter begins sets the precedent for the ensuing relationship. As a woman, you never want to put yourself in a position of having to initiate major milestones in your relationship. This can lead to toxic cycles, because once the foundation is established between two people, it's almost impossible to reverse.

There is no amount of pressure that can convince a man in a one-sided relationship to suddenly step up to the plate, especially when you've assumed that role. A man who desires you for more than just the short term won't hesitate to make his intentions known verbally, and then follow up with action.

Part of being pursued is presenting yourself as *available* to be sought after. This is true, but there has to be balance. If you start a relationship with pursuit of a man, this approach may give you the results you're looking for, at least initially. In fact, it is very likely that this will be the case -- the man will be flattered by a beautiful woman, and he will return the favor. However, as the relationship continues, this initial flattery will begin to taper off. You will start to see the signs of an unhealthy and lopsided relationship: waiting for his next call, always reaching out first, then initiating every major step. When you allow the man to pursue you, it sends a message of your expectation to be sought after. That is the start of a healthy relationship, founded by the basis of a confident and assured mindset.

Whether you have a traditional thought process or lean towards new ways of the world, it's been proven that *most* men are, in fact, hunters. And who are you to stand in the way of their natural instinct? It is biological and evolutionary. No one can honestly say that if a man truly wants something, he won't at least show signs of wanting to pursue it, especially when it comes to women. Some of us are insistent on the idea that it's completely fine to pursue a man, as long as he takes the bait. But, if you pursue a man too much, you can overlook signs that their interest only goes as far as *your* efforts. For instance, if you find yourself in a situation where there is an obvious mutual attraction, but he seems noticeably shy or intimidated by you, there are subtle gestures you can make. Show him that you notice him and that you *want* to be noticed. Make your attraction known, but don't go overboard. Remember, the idea is to present yourself as available to be pursued, not thirsty for attention. If he doesn't make a move after this, then he may not want it badly enough. That's fine. There's no reason to take offense. Save your affection and energy for a man who is enthralled by you, who wants to do whatever is needed to show that you are who he absolutely wants. If a man wants you badly enough, there is simply nothing that can stop him from pursuing what he wants -- not fear of rejection, timidity, or even a previous heartbreak.

Work tirelessly to transform your mindset so you only respond to men who have shown that they undoubtedly want you. There is no question what God intended for women. You do not love a man because you had to approach him and convince him to love you. You love him because he loves you and put his love on display for you. Apply this mindset to your daily life as a woman. I did, and it worked. Not only did it help maintain my self-worth and reduce my anxiety in the romantic arena, but it also allowed me to attract and fall in love with the right man -- who first loved me.

Let Him Acquire You

Your time, affection, and love should be willingly earned from a man. You should never be expected to give in to a man's desires without first being acquired. The word acquired means "to *gain* for oneself through *actions*." Now, you wouldn't allow someone to take your most valuable possession without working for it, right? You, as a woman, are invaluable. Everything you bring to the table, as a woman, is precious and therefore should not be handed over easily. A man that wants to claim you as his own should be willing to do what's necessary to acquire you. Adopting this mindset is as simple as believing you are precious and carrying yourself as though you are. Once a man has taken the steps necessary to win you over and claim you as his own, you have entered the phase of *being acquired*, or in other words, you are *exclusively* dating.

Once you are exclusive you begin spending more time together and learning more intimate things about each other. This is the period when most women exhale and tend to fall in love. That being said, when in the "Acquired" phase you shouldn't find yourself giving so much that your man thinks his work is done. Read that again. Just because he can claim you as his own, does not mean he can put his feet up and get comfortable. Take living together for example. Moving in together often sends your man the message that he has met the end goal, or he has won the prize at the end of the "game." This arrangement may seem convenient, but it can backfire -- he may feel there is no value in pursuing marriage, or even expending more energy to build on your relationship. You could find yourself convincing him that marriage is much more than a piece of paper and a ring. In reality, marriage is the ultimate goal of a loving relationship, a promise that you will stick by each other's side "til death do us part." This is significant. It is the foundation for a family and commitment. It is a result of demonstrated love and support. Commitment is not defined by living together under the same roof, splitting the rent, or acting as if you are married.

Another example of today's culture warping our view of relationships is the idea of a "ride or die chick." Let me be clear: in no instance should a woman make the statement that she will be there no matter what. This concept disregards everything that makes a man want to earn your love. There are conditions in love. The idea that a woman should stick by her man no matter what can set you up for disrespectful treatment because your man will believe "she's not going anywhere." I say this not only so you can attract the right man who will truly cherish you, but so you can avoid extremely toxic relationships that tend to hurt women much more than they do men. Sure men can also be affected by relationships that go south, but they are far less likely to stay in toxic situations than women. This probably explains why you never hear men referred to as "ride or die"-- they seldom play that role.

It's important to know that all of this isn't just some test or game you're playing with men -- these are standards and evidence of your self-worth. Earning a woman's love doesn't stop after she's been acquired. Happiness and longevity are also a direct result of being with a man who understands that you must be cherished.

Once you have been acquired by the right man, you should be all right with being vulnerable in your relationship. It is part of our natural make up as women. While we are innately softer and more vulnerable than men are emotionally, there are times we don't fully display our vulnerability. Often, this is because we see it as a weakness, when in fact it is a strength, an ability to express built-up emotion that could be damaging if kept too long inside. If the man you choose is not being honest and forthright, if he is not being strong as a leader, why would you feel comfortable being vulnerable with him? We are intelligent creatures -- we only show our vulnerability when we feel safe and protected. Put in simpler terms, we, as women, can't play our role if a man does not play his. Just as you want him to pursue you in a relationship and dating, he should be strong and make you feel safe enough to play yours. No woman is going to display her true feelings when she thinks that she may be taken advantage of if she does indeed become vulnerable. Men have to understand that a woman needs to exhale.

We are naturally more caring, emotional, and vulnerable. And though times have changed, who we are at the core has not. Most of us have merely adapted in order to thrive. I'm absolutely guilty of this. For years, I dated men that sometimes refused to treat me with love and respect -- this led me to become hard, tough. I grew tired of my kindness being perceived as weakness, and decided to lead with strength and dominance. No man was ever going to get the best of me. It worked for a while, but it wasn't long before my true emotions took over. Underneath my powerful facade was complete and total vulnerability. After all, I'm a woman; and to be honest, I should be able to be one in all aspects of my life -- especially in love.

One of the main reasons I fell in love with my husband was because he allowed me to be *comfortable* being vulnerable. This is not synonymous with weakness. It just means you can let your guard down and reveal your true heart. I believe all women want to be vulnerable with men. They want to be able to express their raw feelings and emotions. That is part of a woman's role in relationships. But it takes the right man, one who is compassionate, honest, and trustworthy, to bring this out in a woman in this day and age. The world has convinced us that strength, power, and leadership defines the new woman --which, in part, is true. But in love, the roles change. The truth of the matter is that God did not design it to be that way. The Bible clearly states that a man's role is to be a protector and provider. So, if you are a protector, then naturally you are stronger than your partner, the woman.

Still, be careful not to wear your heart on your

sleeve, especially if you have yet to be acquired. In fact, this is exactly the opposite of what I am saying. You want a man in your life who makes you feel comfortable enough to express emotion, whether it be viscerally happy or sad tears. If your man is not allowing you to be vulnerable and open around him, it should be considered a red flag. Feeling comfortable enough in to express any and every emotion is not a desire, it is an essential need, like water or shelter. Choose wisely -- choose a man who listens, comforts, and protects.

Expect to Be Cherished

Being *cherished* is the natural reward once you've made a successful shift by applying the "pursue and acquire" mindset. A man who is truly fit for your love should always desire to and take responsibility for cherishing you. There are no ifs, ands, or buts to this statement. Your man should take effort to keep you happy -- effort he will want to work at, improve upon, and maintain. Notably, this expectation does not mean that you should purposely be difficult or hard to satisfy. It only implies that it is a woman's right to be cherished by her man. Love him and care for him, but don't ever let him feel as if you are a commodity to be taken for granted. He should feel that he has to maintain a certain standard to hold onto your love. You are only a constant in his life as long as he loves and cherishes you.

It is simple human nature to not cherish or value things that don't demand substantial effort to obtain. You don't cherish things that come easily or cheaply. You cherish things that have demanded long and hard work to earn. You cherish the people in your life who are irreplaceable, that you can't imagine life without. You cherish the items you possess that hold value that is more than material or financial. You cherish things that provide you with a sense of love and self-worth.

All of this doesn't mean that men have to do all the work. In fact, it's quite the contrary -- there are different roles for men and women in a relationship. These roles can be flexible, but it is helpful to set in place certain guidelines that apply to the man and the woman. A man should understand that there are always standards to be met. You are someone to be pursued, acquired, consistently loved, and openly cherished. There is no other option for a relationship. Someone must take the lead, and the man is in the best position to do so, biologically, socially, and culturally. Once you let men audition for YOU, instead of auditioning for men, the man you have been long waiting for is right around the corner. It takes a mindset rich with self-love, self-worth, and self-respect. It takes standards. Expect to be pursued, acquired, and cherished. Here are important points to remember:

Mindset Shift Takeaways

Pursued	Acquired	Cherished
Your Takeaways	*Your Takeaways*	*Your Takeaways*
➣ Make your standards known ➣ Don't initiate ➣ Be approachable	➣ Don't get too comfortable ➣ Don't live with him	➣ Expect to be cherished; don't accept anything less ➣ Don't be too difficult to satisfy
His Actions	*His Actions*	*His Actions*
➣ Seek you out ➣ Respect your standards	➣ Continue to gain your affection through effort ➣ Make his intentions clear	➣ Continue to earn your love ➣ Understand true commitment comes with a ring

Habit One Takeaways

- You deserve to be sought after and a man who truly wants you will pursue you. Adopting this mindset will inherently lead to feelings of self-worth, which will attract the right men.
- There are clear steps, stages, and phases to a relationship. Blurring the lines between these lays a rocky foundation. Setting boundaries is essential.

- You are someone who must be cherished. Believe that. When you believe that and exude self-worth, men will understand that you are truly someone to be cherished long term.

Habit One Reflections

1. Think about all of the dating prospects in your life right now. What do you think are the biggest changes you need to make to effectively shift your dating mindset?

_____
_____
_____
_____
_____
_____
_____
_____

2. What are some actions you can put into place today in order to make these changes?

DATING STANDARDS THAT SPEAK

_____
_____
_____
_____
_____
_____
_____
_____

HABIT TWO: LET YOUR STANDARDS SPEAK

Standards lead to either respect or release.

Standards, you know that they are essential to dating, but maybe you're not quite sure where to begin. The first thing to understand is that your standards, on a broad scale, are a true reflection of who you are, what makes you happy, and want you expect out of life. In dating, standards serve as a barometer for how to determine if a man is even dateable. Your standards should be aligned with the vision for *your* happy ending. Every woman has a different image in her mind of the future she desires for herself. Once you are clear about your vision, you can inherently date with the right standards as your foundation.

DATING STANDARDS THAT SPEAK

Take a few minutes to reflect on the way you envision your future -- this is your overall vision. Do you want to be married in the next two years? How many children do you want? Do you want to be a stay-at-home mom? It may seem as though these questions should be asked further in your future. But, the fact is, your answers actually determine the types of men that you should be entertaining in your life. For instance, if you plan to be married within the next few years, dating a man who is not interested in settling down is not a smart choice. Align your standards with the picture you have in mind for your life. Later, you'll use those standards to determine the qualities and characteristics you should be looking for in a man. Describe the overall vision for your future:

_____
_____
_____
_____
_____
_____
_____
_____

These days there are so many skewed perspectives on

standards. Some think women need to get their head out of the clouds and lower their standards, while others believe high standards actually hold us back. But you know that as long as your standards are aligned and realistic they will attract the right men. With women becoming more and more successful in this day and age, there is absolutely nothing wrong with wanting a man who complements what you bring to the table. That's not too much to ask, is it?

Part of setting your standards is understanding the core elements a man should fulfill. A man should satisfy a woman in four key areas: mentally, physically, financially, and morally.

Mentally & Emotionally	Physically	Financially	Morally
A man should make you feel emotionally safe and comfortable being vulnerable.	He should be your protector and also satisfy your intimate needs (once he has earned your affection).	A man should be capable and willing to provide for you monetarily.	His character and integrity are essential. Consider the kind of potential husband and father he would be.

Now that you have captured your vision, use the key areas above to align your standards. There are practical ways to develop and build the right standards in the dating arena. They begin with shifting your mindset about yourself and what you deserve. They also include understanding the dynamic you have with the men you are dating. It's important to understand that not every man you fall for will meet your standards. This is why alignment between your vision and your standards is so vital. You can fall for just about any man if you spend enough time with him -- even if he doesn't measure up. The fact is, there really is something to love about everyone, no matter how many red flags they bring to the table. If you spend enough time with someone, you may begin to feel attached to them, especially if things become physical or intimate. But is this what you really want? Don't settle. What starts as a meaningless fling, can easily turn into attachment. Then, it can become difficult to detach. The goal is to avoid this. Something that begins with no real purpose -- that isn't serious -- has very little chance of turning into a long-lasting relationship.

Based on your vision, what are your dating standards? Do require a man to be established in his career? Should his five-year plan include a wife and children? Are you fine with a man who still enjoys late nights at the club? Write down standards that align to your vision:

_____

_____

_____

_____

_____

_____

_____

_____

The best way to set a foundation for a relationship that you will want to hold onto and nurture is to set clear standards and intentions early in the dating process. Part of this process involves identifying which characteristics you are looking for in a man and making the best dating decisions based on those traits. This may take time, but waiting for the right man is a far better option than settling for man after man and bad relationship after bad relationship. This is simply a waste of time -- it doesn't do anything for you. In fact, settling for this cycle can be detrimental to your social and emotional well-being.

Once you understand the real value of your standards, you also have to be careful not to hold them over a man's head unfairly. Yes, men should meet your standards, but it is *your* responsibility to make them known. You can not expect a man to come up to a level that you haven't set. That would be like a teacher giving a student an exam without first providing a study guide. This can be a set-up for failure, and you want to give them a fair shot. Recognize that just as you have dated different men throughout your life, he has dated several women before you. And, trust me, each and every one of them has presented a unique perspective on what is acceptable and what is not. There is nothing wrong with this at all. The idea is to allow your standards to set you apart -- just make sure you go about it in the right way.

There are also unspoken ways you can make your standards known to a man. In fact, this is the best way to gain insight into whether or not a particular man is dating material. It allows you to bypass some of the awkward, direct questions and solely observe his actions. For instance, if your expectation is that a man calls you at least a week in advance to plan a date with you, but he calls a day before -- that certainly doesn't meet your standards. So, how do you respond? By telling him that you feel disrespected by his last minute attempt to secure your time? Or do you opt to go on the date, then have a negative attitude the entire time? No need to make him feel bad. It's not necessarily his fault. Afterall, I'm sure there are plenty of women out there who wouldn't even flinch at such behavior. There are better ways to put him on the right track. Take a few notes from this scenario:

When Nichelle met David, a good looking guy who worked in her office building, she wasn't sure if they would hit it off. Especially since so many other women in her company had eyes for him. Still, she still found him to be smart, successful, and handsome. But, when he approached her on a Wednesday hoping to have dinner with her on Friday -- she wasn't having it. I mean, who did he think he was dealing with, right? Wrong. She politely explained that she already had plans for the weekend, which, by the way wasn't true. In fact, she was very available and would really like to see if they could possibly be a good match. Except she had been down the "last minute date road" without success and wasn't in a rush to make the same mistake. The next week, David tried the same thing, this time reaching out on Thursday for a lunch date on Saturday. So, she was more transparent in her response, "I usually plan my weekend a week in advance, but maybe next time." That struck a nerve with him, because the very next day he asked her to pencil him in for next Saturday night. Bam!

You see, standards speak volumes -- even when unspoken. By holding to your standards you can teach men how you expect to be treated. The right man will make the necessary adjustments to his usual behavior to meet your expectations.

At the same time, be aware that making your standards known may reduce your dating options. Regardless, having fewer options should *not* impact your willingness to uphold your standards. Standards will always lead either to *respect* or to *release*. Be prepared for some of the men who have expressed interest to suddenly fall off when you begin holding them accountable to your expectations. On the flip side, you'll witness some dating prospects stepping up with greater interest and effort. When you date a man who respects your standards and boundaries, it's often a sign of his genuine interest. He's not in a rush to get what he came for and move on to the next woman. Again, some men will throw in the towel early, which is absolutely fine. Don't be disturbed by men who choose to walk away from you and your values. Let them go, because you don't want to waste your time. It's much better to know early that a relationship won't work than to find out two years down the line. Reserve your time and energy for the men who are willing to work for your attention because those are the ones who will stick around. As long as your standards are aligned and realistic, allow them to speak for you.

Don't Respond to Lukewarm

When my husband and I first started dating, he sat me down and asked me if I wanted to get more serious. It was cute and genuine, but I wasn't sure what he was really asking. "Do you mean a commitment?" I asked. "Well, not just yet, but I would like to head in that direction," he responded. "Oh alright, that's sweet; but let's just wait until we get to that point. In the meantime, let's not put a label on it." No attitude, no irritation -- though unspoken, my response made it clear that I only responded to absolutes. I set my standard, I wasn't willing to accept lukewarm. In other words, I wasn't willing to relinquish my single status, and get too emotionally involved until he was absolutely certain that he was all in. Now, I couldn't blame him for trying. He had been dating women with lower standards, so he didn't know any better at the time. Just four days later, he took me to dinner and asked me for a committed, exclusive relationship. Standards speak volumes.

Don't ever respond to lukewarm. Ladies, you deserve someone who knows what he wants from you. It takes time for a man to realize exactly the type of future he envisions with you. The important thing to understand is that when a man is lukewarm towards you -- meaning he seems to like you, but has yet to express his true intentions -- tread lightly. If he meets all the great qualities you desire in your ideal man, continue to date him and see how things progress. Just be smart about it. Remember, his job is to pursue and acquire you, so keep your emotions in check, and don't do anything that will cause you to fall for him before he's fallen for you.

The fact remains, he should lead in all aspects of the dating and relationship progression. Allow yourself to be pursued. Once he opens up about his feelings and expresses his desire to take things to the next level, then and only then, do you take his hand. If you're not ready, or don't feel the same, speak your mind. If he has long term plans for the two of you, he will respect your honesty and be willing to work even harder to win your love.

When I was dating, I would always make it clear that I would, under no circumstances, accept lukewarm. The Bible reminds us in Revelation that "because you are lukewarm, and neither hot nor cold, I will reject you with disgust." The intention is clear -- if you want me, you must commit fully to me; otherwise I'll move on to the next. This does not mean that he should open up his heart, and lay it on the line for you, in the first few dates. It only means that for you to take him seriously, he must clearly express his intentions to even earn your attention.

Not responding to lukewarm intentions also means that you don't accept unclear or vague messages in general. These sorts of messages most likely mean that he doesn't know what he wants from you or from life. You are in the era of true feminism. You no longer have time to waste daydreaming and fantasizing about mixed messages that a man sends you, when you could be making life moves.

Maintain Your Position

Once we become more serious with a man, we are sometimes less likely to lead with our standards. Our feelings tend to consume our entire being, enabling the man who holds our heart to control our thoughts, actions, and most importantly, our emotions. Much of this distress can be avoided if you learn how to maintain your position when dating. What position do I speak of?

As I mentioned before, the natural, biological roles of men and women were designed to be the hunter and the pursued, the leader and the supporter. Effective relationships generally begin with respect to this design, but tend to change as the relationship progresses. The trick is to maintain the place of being "the pursued," even after you've become emotionally attached.

It may seem natural to constantly want to please the man you're with, but this should not come at your own expense. Keep in mind that when you first meet a man, he is polite, reliable, and always puts his best foot forward in trying to impress you. If he is capable of this behavior early on, he should certainly be able to maintain it once the two of you have settled into a relationship. However, it is largely up to you to maintain the position of being sought after.

Maintaining your position sets the foundation for what keeps women happy and stress-free in their love lives. Think of it like respect -- it dictates how you are viewed and treated in nearly every aspect of the relationship. And much like respect, once you lose it, you'll find yourself in a constant battle to win it back. That battle can soon become bouts of trying to muscle or manipulate your man into doing things that he would ordinarily do without question. Don't misunderstand what I'm saying here. I'm not implying that your relationship is a power struggle, because there is no place for a power struggle in love. But the truth is that a man who cares for you should always put effort towards making you happy. This truth applies from the very first date throughout your relationship, and eventually to marriage. The best way to ensure you are always sought after is to never chase. Pay close attention to this aspect of your relationship, because it is very easy to tip the scale and find yourself working overtime to earn his affection.

As you become more comfortable with one another, you may notice a few of his positive attributes slacking off slightly. Maybe he stops calling you on his way home, or begins checking in on you less often throughout the day. If this happens, you will have the strong urge to do anything possible to draw closer to him. Don't. Ignore your instinct to call him or send repeat texts. Focus on your daily activities and keep yourself busy. This can be a challenge, especially if you're accustomed to talking to him multiple times a day. A good rule of thumb is to leave your cell phone in your car when you go to the grocery store or mall so you won't be tempted to contact him. When you finally do hear from him, act as if you didn't even notice the change in his behavior. Don't even mention it. You are unbothered and too busy to notice. Trust me, it won't be long before he recognizes that the sweet and simple gestures he used to acquire you are necessary to keep your interest. And, if he isn't willing to step up his game to get things back on track, then he must not truly be concerned about losing you. Either way, you will find out where you both stand.

Maintaining your position is vital to keeping a confident headspace, because without it you may find yourself overwhelmed with constant concerns regarding his feelings. If you maintain your position, you'll never have to ponder these thoughts, because his constant pursuit will inherently make his intentions clear. Just remember that when a man truly wants you, he is never hesitant to make it known. And as a grown, amazing woman, you have no need to desire any man who expects you to chase him. Of course, no one wants a man who wears his feelings on his sleeve; but a real man makes his purpose for the relationship unquestionable.

So, how do you ensure your position? First, don't settle for any situation that makes you feel uncomfortable. No man is going to be perfect, and sometimes it can be difficult to weigh flaws. But not for you anymore, right? Just refer to your Ideal Man List and be loyal to it. You don't want to end up like Robin:

Robin was in a two year relationship with Lyle, who constantly referred to her as "the one." His actions rarely matched his words, but she loved him, so she held onto hope of a future with him. Then, one day out of the blue he decided to take a part-time job as a bouncer at a local club. Ordinarily, his choice may not seem like a deal breaker, but in the past, his night-life "activities" had caused so many problems in their relationship. She begged him to leave the job. He refused and promised that he could handle the late nights of temptation, if she would only compromise. Rather than pulling away from the relationship knowing the situation was a deal breaker for her, she spent the next six months crying, constantly going through his phone, and stalking his social media. The man that had once called her "the one" wasn't even returning her calls anymore. She had lost her position -- and at the same time, herself.

Knowing when to use your heart and when to use your head is key when trying to maintain your position. You should never plead with your man to refrain from doing something that you are dead set against. In pursuing you, it should always be his goal to please *you*. So, take notice if a man is constantly disappointing you. It can only mean one of two things: either he is not legitimately concerned with your happiness, or he is incapable of meeting your expectations. Whichever is true, both are notable reasons to reconsider your compatibility as a pair and the future of the relationship.

You should understand the difference between situations that are worth compromising and those that are straight up deal breakers. Compromise in love is when two people find a middle ground in a situation or disagreement. Outcomes that benefit only one person in the relationship, and have the potential to leave the other person hurt or uncomfortable are signs of an unhealthy partnership. A man who loves you will not want to put you in a space that is knowingly upsetting to you and the stability of the relationship.

Keep in mind that everyone experiences disappointment or unhappiness at some point in relationships. Anytime two individuals come together with the intention of growing together, disagreements are inevitable -- as is compromise. Just remember, ladies, compromise is not synonymous with lowering your standards.

Habit Two Takeaways

- It is your responsibility to make your standards known to a man -- whether spoken or unspoken.
- You want to attract men who are willing to work to meet your standards. Be prepared

for some men to walk away from you once you make your standards known. Not everyone will be up for the challenge.
- Maintaining your position in a relationship is vital to keeping a confident headspace with men.

Habit Two Reflections

1. Based on your standards, what are the main characteristics you should avoid in men that you date?

_____
_____
_____
_____
_____
_____
_____
_____

2. Can you think of a past situation when you could have used an unspoken lesson to teach a man your standards?

DATING STANDARDS THAT SPEAK

_____
_____
_____
_____
_____
_____
_____
_____

HABIT THREE: CAPTURE YOUR VISION

Your ideal man should be aligned with the overall vision for your life.

The overall vision you have identified for your future is an excellent starting point to understanding the type of man you want to attract into your life. The next piece is to break down the qualities that will best compliment your version of happily ever after. Now it's time to put your ideal man on paper. Capture your vision. This way you always have a visual of exactly what you are looking for in a man. Have your sights set on your standards and when something jumps out as a red flag, it will be because your expectations are ingrained. Once you create your list, refer to it time and time again, and tweak it

DATING STANDARDS THAT SPEAK

as you date and learn more about what you want. Then, dating any man who doesn't possess many of your desired qualities or displays traits that you have deemed deal breakers will become increasingly unlikely.

This secret worked wonders for me. My husband is far from perfect, but I'm still amazed how much he embodies the qualities I wrote on my list. First, pinpoint the vision of your ideal man, keeping in mind that what you desire should be aligned with the overall vision and standards that you created in the previous chapters. Write down specifically what you need and desire in a man. Writing things down makes them concrete, allowing you to see them take shape, stick in your mind, and serve as a guide. I'm sure you've heard stories about people like Oprah and Steve Harvey who have done vision boards with tremendous success, right? This exercise works exactly the same way. I kept my list in my bible near the scripture Habakkuk 2:2 to *write the vision and make it plain*.

One of the best ways to document the qualities that you long for in a husband is to make a list that highlights *Desired Qualities* (good to have, but negotiable) and *Deal Breakers* (non-negotiable). If you are struggling, refer to your list of standards in a man. Surely at the top of your list are those qualities that are most important to you, right? And, qualities that threaten your overall vision should be marked as absolute deal breakers.

Be sure to be realistic and not superficial with your list. When you place too much emphasis on externally attractive qualities that are front and center during the early dating phase, you overlook the deal breakers that may be hiding in plain sight. Otherwise, you'll find yourself picking a man solely based on his physical traits. This approach could allow more important factors to go undetected until it's too late. So, whether your deal breakers are religious faith, how much he earns for a living, or how many children he has, the most important thing to realize is that once a deal breaker is revealed -- you must understand the importance of pulling back from the situation. Continuing to date him after this point will likely lead to a pattern of unsuccessfully trying to change him, or struggling internally to accept qualities outside of, or below, your standards.

Now that you understand the benefits of capturing your ideal man on paper, are you willing to adopt this habit as your own? Draft your own list of desired qualities and deal breakers below. Remember, be specific.

DATING STANDARDS THAT SPEAK

Your Ideal Man

Desired Qualities	Deal Breakers
☐ _____	☐ _____
☐ _____	☐ _____
☐ _____	☐ _____
☐ _____	☐ _____
☐ _____	☐ _____
☐ _____	☐ _____
☐ _____	☐ _____
☐ _____	☐ _____
☐ _____	☐ _____
☐ _____	☐ _____
☐ _____	☐ _____
☐ _____	☐ _____

Everything you are accomplishing here is action-oriented. This activity is the opposite of being lazy and careless in the dating game, but your work doesn't stop here. You must also understand ways to learn more about the man who could potentially be a part of your life. If you are truly taking yourselves and the dating scene seriously, then you will want to discover more about each other. Have you ever had a friend who met a man, quickly fell for him, but had no idea what college he graduated from, or even his hometown? You would think that personal facts like this would be one of the first questions asked, but too often they are easily skirted. It is wonderful to be able to have a fun, light-hearted time with a potential significant other, but more important to know the core of their being and experiences.

It is ideal for men to initiate spending time with you. However, you should feel led to discuss topics that are important to you. Often, men won't go there, so it's up to you. Initiate the conversation around what matters most to you and be willing to share, as well. All of this is part of dating with standards. Be intentional and you will find yourself wasting less time on dates with men who aren't a potential match for you. Be purposeful for yourself, and be intentional with your time.

For example, if you listed *not ready for marriage* as a deal breaker on your list, then it's essential to ask the right questions early in the dating phase. A man's readiness for a committed, long-lasting relationship often depends on his life experiences. A simple, but effective way to judge a man's experiences in life is to check these two boxes:

☐ *Has he lived alone? Has he been completely independent and entirely selfish for a period of time?*

☐ *Has he experienced the wild phase and got it out of his system? Has he dated around for a time, and is he now ready to "settle down"?*

If the answers are yes, then it is far more likely that he is ready to take dating seriously, and take you seriously.

The purpose of capturing your overall vision, listing your standards, and aligning them with your ideal man is to put you in the best position to attract quality men into your life. This will make your dating options more potential and lead to the man that will become your happily ever after.

Habit Three Takeaways

- The ideal qualities of your potential husband should align to your overall vision and standards.
- Understand that deal breakers should be non-negotiable traits.
- Identify questions that will lead to your

understanding of a man meeting your desired qualities.

Habit Three Reflections

1. Think back to a past relationship that ended badly. Can you recall the reasons why things didn't work out. Write them down, then add them to your list.

_____
_____
_____
_____
_____
_____
_____
_____

2. What are some questions you could ask on a date that would help you learn whether a man meets your criteria?

_____
_____
_____

DATING STANDARDS THAT SPEAK

_____
_____
_____
_____
_____

HABIT FOUR: BECOME YOUR EXPECTATIONS

You should be a representative of what you are looking for in a man.

Knowing what to expect from a man can be difficult, unless you have built your expectations around your standards. Elevating your expectations of what a potential husband looks like, as well as being realistic in your overall expectations, determines who you will end up with. No, you should not lower your standards -- as long as they are aligned and realistic. You should, in fact, raise them; but standards and expectations should not be one-sided. You have to take some accountability, too. As a general rule, what you expect from a man should not too far exceed what you bring to the table yourself.

DATING STANDARDS THAT SPEAK

Ladies, we're out here making bigger moves than ever, purchasing our own homes, driving our dream cars, and some of us are even running our own businesses. So, there's absolutely nothing wrong with wanting a man who is on the same level. You don't want to sell yourself short when it comes to who you allow into your world. Maintain high standards when choosing who to share your life with -- but take inventory to ensure that you are being realistic in your expectations. First, you have to ensure that you don't place too much emphasis on a man's external attributes. Of course, we all want someone who's attractive, well put together, and earning a substantial income; but these things can't be the primary factors in your selection process. Understand that his six pack, flashy, new car, and lifestyle can all be fleeting -- or even worse, a well-manicured facade. Differentiating what is important and what is not is essential to developing your standards and expectations. So, what should you be looking for?

One of the first things you should be looking for is character. What are the principles that he lives by? Does he display integrity in his daily decisions and actions? I like to define character as who you are when no one else is looking. There is so much truth to this statement. And that is essentially what you want to learn about the man that you could potentially be sharing your life with. Pay close attention to the areas of his life that may not include you. While he may be putting his best foot forward around you, if he has a crazy, disgruntled ex-girlfriend, or can't seem to get along with anyone in his family, these are likely signs of traits that he may be keeping from you. Just ask Stacey.

Stacey and Kelvin had been dating for just two months when she first saw his ex-girlfriend (and son's mother), Tori, in action. Tori seemed devious and determined to do anything to make him miserable, so Stacey looked to Kelvin for answers. He insisted that Tori was out of her mind and couldn't accept the fact that they were over. As the relationship progressed, the constant drama began to take a toll on their dynamic as a couple. The final straw was when he cancelled a romantic weekend getaway after Tori informed him of a "last minute" recital at his son's school. Stacey knew the only way to move forward with him was to get all three of them on the same page. For the first time she spoke to Tori directly -- and she couldn't believe what she found out. Turns out Kelvin had given her plenty of reasons to act crazy, because he was still sleeping with her! Lesson learned.

Consistency is also an important part of character. With social media and dating apps at their fingertips, men can be easily distracted. One minute, he's sending texts with a quick reply and planning his next date with you. Next, he seems to be a ghost. Then, you don't hear from him for several days. Behavior like this is a symptom of a larger problem with inconsistency. Don't overlook this type of behavior and remember -- men make time for what they truly want.

A man's work ethic speaks volumes about his character. Is he ambitious and focused? Does he keep his word and honor his commitments? Early on, this can be measured by simple actions like calling you back when he promises, or actually being honest about where he is going Saturday night, without you feeling like you have to check on him. Does he exhibit self control? That is an extremely important factor. For instance, does he have multiple children by multiple women? If so, this may be a clear sign that he lacks self control, or, at the very least, lacks the necessary judgment to prevent situations like this. On a smaller scale, take note of hints regarding his level of integrity like keeping his word and taking accountability for his actions -- not just as they relate to you personally, but with his job, friends, or even paying the bills on time. How does he treat the waiter on your dates? Is he polite, does he tip well? All of these small, everyday actions provide insight into who he is internally -- his character. The man you ultimately end up with should bring out the very best in you. And having a man with solid character plays a major role in achieving your best self.

Here are a few examples of questions that will help you determine the true integrity of a man. Each of these qualities represent signs of someone with morals and integrity.

Integrity Checklist

- [ ] *Does he tip well at restaurants?*
- [ ] *Is he respectful to the other women in his life?*
- [ ] *Does he pay bills on time?*
- [ ] *Do mutual acquaintances have good things to say about him?*
- [ ] *Does he have a good reputation at his job?*
- [ ] *Does he get along well with his siblings?*
- [ ] *Is he accountable for his mistakes?*

As you lay out your personal expectations for

men, you also must be realistic about who you are and the attributes you bring to a relationship. Believe it or not, men are also looking for specific desirable qualities in the women they choose to add to their lives. Most are not just wandering aimlessly, dating whoever they seem to be attracted to at the time. It's wrong to assume that all men are just out here looking for a good time. So, before you wave a flag saying, "I want a man who is settled, and can make me a good home cooked meal!" make sure *your* version of a home cooked meal isn't take-out from the five-star restaurant down the street from your house. You should be a representative of what you are looking for in a man. So, take a good, long look at yourself before you start insisting that your dream man has thousands of dollars laying around in his bank account just waiting to spend on you. Be realistic. If you insist on the lavish life, but you're living check to check because you can't control your obsession with luxury brands, you're not being fair to your potential partner.

The bottom line is that having realistic expectations does not necessarily mean lowering your standards, but it does require shifting them to fit your own characteristics. You simply cannot expect highly sought after qualities and traits from him that you don't possess yourself. So return to your Ideal Man

List and remember to be realistic when selecting your desired qualities. But first, let's test your insight on expectations. Choose your top three attributes you would want in a man from the list below.

Attributes Checklist

- ☐ Makes you smile daily
- ☐ Great father to his kids
- ☐ Owns his home
- ☐ Vacations frequently
- ☐ Mom is his best friend
- ☐ Honest and loyal
- ☐ Loves to cook

Standards and expectations should be specific to your vision, so as long as you selected *honest and loyal* from the list you're on the right track.

Just as we have to shift our mindset and present ourselves as available to be pursued, we also need to prepare ourselves to be acquired. No man in his right mind wants a woman who doesn't take care of herself, her home, or her finances. A man does not want to be with a woman who he constantly has to bail out before they are even married, just like you don't want to take care of him like a child. Sure, you probably live alone and pay your own bills, but are you living a lifestyle that aligns with the vision you have for your future? If you expect a certain quality from a man, then it's ideal that you possess that quality yourself.

I am always hearing incessant complaints from men saying that women these days don't cook, rarely clean, and place too much emphasis on material things. Ouch! But, is there any truth to this? Ladies, start preparing yourself to be settled. Make your home -- no matter the size -- your castle, where you prepare fancy dinners and wine for yourself. You have to start somewhere. Where you invest your time also matters. How can you turn your nose up at him for spending too much time at clubs when you spend three nights a week at Happy Hour with your friends? It's perfectly fine to hang out with the girls, but if you want a homebody, you should mirror those qualities in your own life. You can't constantly say you want to meet a man in a bookstore or grocery store when you don't frequent those places. You have to become what you are hoping to attract. Like attracts like.

And please, be mindful when you consider dating men who only have the *potential* to meet your standards. Take a good, hard look at the big picture. Do his words and actions send the same message? For instance, if a man works in sales, claims his goal is to run his own IT company; yet you never see him working towards that goal. That does not qualify as potential. Someone with potential displays tangible evidence of progression. Trust your instincts. God gave women intuition for a reason. In the same way that you try to mirror the qualities that you want to find in a husband, a man should mirror the qualities that you want in him through his actions. Be aware and trust yourself.

POTENTIAL = ACTION + PROGRESSION

Habit Four Takeaways

- A man who is surrounded by drama and chaos is likely the author of it.
- You should be a representative of your standards and expectations. You can not

expect what you are not capable of becoming.
- Potential is an action. Listen to a man's goals, beliefs, and expectations, and watch for actions that align with his words.

Habit Four Reflections

1. List a few characteristics you desire in a man, but don't necessarily possess at the moment.

_____
_____
_____
_____
_____
_____
_____
_____

2. What are some changes you can make in your life to be a better representation of your own expectations?

_____

JANTAE RASHAUN

HABIT FIVE: CURB YOUR ATTRACTIONS

What you need in a man and what we are attracted to can be two entirely different things.

As a woman, you normally have no issue articulating the qualities you deem necessary in the man of your dreams. But somehow, someway, you find yourself dating the same type of man over and over again, someone who has nothing in common with the vision in your mind of the ideal man for you. You struggle through a bad relationship, muster up the strength to end it, then convince yourself that you've learned a lesson from Mr. Wrong. So you get back out into the dating world, only to end up falling for the *next* Mr. Wrong, despite the clear red flags, and have the audacity to wonder why you end up back at square one. We ask ourselves "What am I doing wrong?" like it's not our fault, but let's be honest -- sometimes, it is. Often, the qualities you know you need in a partner, and what you are instinctively attracted to, can be two entirely different things. You may say you want a man who is ready to settle down, but then date someone who clearly states that he's not looking for anything serious. You set yourself up to fight an uphill battle when you ignore obvious red flags. It may not be easy to accept, but this behavior means you have to drastically change what you're attracted to, ladies.

Embracing this resolve may seem like an impossible task, but it truly isn't. We've all been in a situation that has caused our minds and God-given female intuition to fail us. How many times have you met a man who is by no means relationship material, but you are uncontrollably attracted to him for all the wrong reasons? Exactly! There's nothing more difficult than telling yourself "No" when every other part of your body is screaming "Yes."

Latrice was fresh out of a three year relationship that left her with a scorned heart and a tainted view of men. She vowed to spend the next year hanging out with her friends and living her best life. Until one night she met Marcus, sexy, mysterious and all together everything she would avoid under usual circumstances. But, since she wasn't looking for love -- she indulged. She spent the next six months caught up in a cloud of great sex accompanied by jealous fits of rage, thanks to constant phone calls from random women. Still somehow, she continued to ask herself if she could fit this man, with absolutely nothing to offer (besides sex), into her well-planned future. Needless to say, the relationship didn't work out. Lucky girl.

Whether it's his relentless charm, or the way he swaggers into a room with his chest puffed, or his bedroom eyes that make you want to do things that you know you shouldn't, there's no denying that there are men like this just waiting to take advantage. Maybe you have already gone down that road, or maybe you are there at this very moment in time. In these instances, the answer is simple: your emotions are being driven by passion. This is not what a lasting relationship is built on. Of course, ladies, you all want passion and strong physical attraction -- that is inherent, because you probably wouldn't even date someone who you aren't attracted to in the first place. Though it is definitely not a negative emotion, you have to be mindful when it comes to passion. Passion shouldn't be what entices you to want to have a man in your life, but rather, it should be the product of two compatible people who have grown to desire each other. Relationships that are built on seeds of passion instead of substance are bound to fail. Passion in this instance can lead to emotional and physical vulnerability. Pair these traits with a weak foundation, and it's a vicious cycle.

Oh, the dreaded cycle. We've all been in relationships in which the one constant was the break-ups and make-ups. He keeps messing up, you keep forgiving him and taking him back, and through all the drama, it becomes harder and harder to let him go. Sound familiar?

Sometimes you may not realize this is what is occurring. You may be so lost in the romance and passion of the relationship that you don't even consider that it may be unhealthy. In this case, reassess the situation you are in. Ask yourself honest questions and be truthful in your answers. Are you constantly asking yourself, "Will he call? Is he still seeing other women? What did that conversation last night really mean?" These may be signs of a relationship built on the wrong qualities. Riding an emotional rollercoaster can be entrancing and exhilarating. But in no case is it healthy or stable, which are prerequisites for any relationship expected to last long term.

To change your attractions, you first have to know the qualities to avoid. There are often clear signs that you may or may not find attractive that are absolute deal breakers. And, there are also qualities in men that you may overlook, even though they are signs of an ability to love, respect, and cherish you. Let's discuss what to avoid and what qualities to shift your attractions towards.

What to Avoid

As for tangible signs of being unavailable, do not date married men or even newly separated men. Don't even think about it. If a man is in a marriage, or has recently walked away from a long marriage, he is not entirely emotionally available. He may try to convince you how awful his marriage is. He may tell you that he wants out, but for some reason he just can't escape or divorce right now. These are not good explanations. First of all, it is never morally right to date a married man. Second, there is no chance it will move past sexual intimacy or simple fun. If he has separated from his wife and is still expressing interest, move forward at your own risk, but be vigilant and aware -- you could have a long, difficult road ahead of you.

Understand that men who are recently divorced

can be difficult to read. A bad marriage and stressful divorce can be extremely mentally and emotionally taxing, especially if there are kids involved. And most importantly, don't be too willing to relinquish your time, energy, and heart.

When it comes to married men, they always try to conceal the truth for as long as possible. So, be watchful for potential red flags. Look for these telltale signs if you suspect that the man you are dating may be married:

1. He is a text king. If texting is his preferred means of communication with you, really begin to evaluate why. Men can send a text from *anywhere* at *anytime*, sitting next to *anyone*. Let that sink in for a minute.
2. He is Mr. 9 to 5. When a man's most available hours seem to be morning and afternoon, and he suddenly goes silent in the early evening hours, he may be hiding something about his personal life.
3. He has a ring finger fade. The most obvious sign, but you'd be surprised how many women overlook this. It only takes a second to sneak a peek during your first encounter, or even first date. Consider this sign old faithful -- it will never lie.

Take Tasha, for instance:

Tasha, while freelancing for an entertainment company, met a co-worker named Mike whom she instantly hit it off with. And he felt the same way. He relentlessly went after her despite her reluctance to become involved with someone she worked with. She tried to stave it off, but eventually gave into his charm and her feelings. Instantly, he was candid about his separation from his wife, so she didn't let it affect their passionate relationship. Like clockwork, Mike would call her at 8:00 a.m. to say good morning and they would chat frequently throughout the day. Though they lived in different cities, business trips allowed them to spend plenty of quality time together. Then, one morning, he didn't call. He didn't respond to her calls all morning. Then, later that evening, a call came from his number. When she answered, though, she was confronted by a voice that wasn't his. "I'm Mike's wife," the woman said.

What to Find Attractive

The bottom line is this: don't base your life around a man who is not truly there for you. Physical attraction is great, ladies, but it can be found in much more whole and constant places. Attraction can be borne from love. You will never get to where you are supposed to be in life if you are always in a relationship full of passionate ups and downs, taking you into a storm of meaningless arguments, worries, and anxiety. This gets you nowhere. Many women make the mistake of thinking that relationships are full of valleys and peaks. This may be true, but they don't occur frequently. In a relationship with a sturdy foundation, there can still be peaks. There can still be those amazing moments when you feel on top of the world. The difference is that you will always feel loved, and you will need to put in the work before you reach them. A true peak is more satisfying than an artificial one. A true peak turns calmly down, and valleys are few and far between. I'm guilty of ignoring red flags, not trusting my intuition, and staying in relationships long past their expiration date. And yes, I learned from them; but ladies, come on! There are much better ways to learn -- like reading this book, for example.

You need someone who appreciates you, builds you up, motivates you, and is a constant source of love. Yes, you may go through ups and downs with your future husband, but he should not be the cause of them -- he should help you both get through them. Predictable is a word with a negative, boring connotation, but a healthy relationship should be predictable in a sense. You shouldn't have to second guess whether he will keep his promise to call or take you to dinner next weekend. Love should be reliable and consistent, not fleeting. There is no replacement for the love of a man who will be there for you when you need him. That is the basis of true commitment. There can never be a long-lasting relationship borne solely out of physical attraction.

Start finding qualities like intelligence, sensitivity, and selflessness attractive. Notice a kind smile rather than a great body. Fall in love with his mind, the curious look in a man's eyes, or the way he seems to care when he is talking to you. These are all things you, as a woman, have good intuition about. They should be the first things you notice, so let this be what attracts you! If you change what you are initially looking for, you will find the right man, along with the burning love and passion you desire. All you have to do is align your standards and put the habits in this book to use. The more you date below your standards and fall for the wrong men, though, the more difficult your dating life will be.

Change your attractions from the passion-filled rollercoaster lover to the man who will put in the work needed to acquire and cherish you. Make a list of all the good qualities that you should be looking harder for in men, and do away with the negative

Choose Compatibility Over Passion

There is a clear distinction between compatibility and passion. Compatibility can lead to passion -- in fact, it's an overarching producer of passion. But passion, on the other hand, almost never produces compatibility. It just doesn't work that way. It's also possible that what you have identified as passion is actually something more detrimental. Drastic highs and lows, for example, can easily be mistaken for passion. Again, you have all been there. You spend a hot whirlwind of a weekend with your man that leaves you on an emotional high. Throughout the next week, the calls and texts flow regularly, until all of a sudden it's Friday and you don't hear a word from him. Anxiety begins to set in as his texts become more sporadic and vague, sending you into a tailspin of confusion. After a lonely weekend hoping to hear back from him, you finally receive the "Good morning, beautiful" text on Monday morning, and you are suddenly back in it, like a simple flip of a switch. He comes over saying and doing all the things he knows will rope you right back in --and just like that, you're on another high. That is until the next unforeseen, but somehow not unexpected plummet. Ladies, take my word for it -- this is not passion. It is instability disguised as romantic passion. This pattern may be exhilarating and some women don't even realize they're drawn to the feeling. But it keeps you tied-down in relationships that are bound for failure.

Not only are drastic extremes, like passion followed by heartbreak, in a relationship a sign that you are on the wrong dating path, but they chip away slowly at your self-esteem and perception of what love is -- two components of the mindset that needs to be shifted in the opposite direction to take you from single to sought after. Self-worth and an understanding of what love truly is are the most essential mindset shifts, and being caught in a vicious relationship cycle with no happy medium is counteractive to the mindset shift you want to promote. The types of behavior that promote these peaks and valleys produce insecurity, guilt, and shame. Shaky and inconsistent communication, lack of trust, and unstable emotions -- these are all unconducive to a healthy relationship. They are the types of behaviors that leave you feeling insecure and lost down in the valley of a relationship waiting to return to some sort of peak.

Now, it's very likely that you all went through something like this in your twenties, the age when men haven't matured enough to get past "playing the field," or are still experiencing the types of scenarios that they must go through to learn what it takes to be in a lasting relationship. So, don't be discouraged. There are still men out there who have the mindset needed for a serious relationship with the ultimate goal of marriage. If you don't find someone right away, wait it out -- learn about yourself, prepare your own mindset for that undertaking. Women tend to be much more prepared to find "the one," which makes it hard for young women who are looking for serious relationships. It can be extremely difficult to resist the temptation of a man who is at a different level of maturity, and it can also be difficult to tell whether he is mature enough to work towards marriage or not. It can also be difficult to resist the temptation of a man who is not ready for a serious relationship but stokes a lot of passion between the two of you. One of the biggest reasons women say they don't like a "nice" guy is because of the lack of passion, the lack of fire. But in reality these men may just not show this side of them as easily as men who are not perfectly nice. Or this passion may be shown in different ways. For example, a nice guy may always be there when you need to call him, offer to take you out to dinner unexpectedly, take care of you when you're sick, and be there through the ups and downs -- not be the cause of the ups and downs.

Kira and Corey had been in an on and off relationship for three years. Kira felt like she could spend the rest of her life with him, even though they never seemed to go more than a few months without breaking up. When things were good, they did everything together and Corey was always showing her affection and expressing his love. They were inseparable. But then, the smallest thing would trigger an explosive argument and it was as if the seasons would change like the flip of a switch. He would just sink into his own space and wouldn't call or come around anymore. He changed to hanging out with his friends and spending late nights out doing who knows what. But, it wasn't the same for Kira. She would repeatedly call him, trying to figure out his thought process and why he was being so distant, but would get nothing in return. Just when she came to her darkest point, all of a sudden -- he would hop back in. It wasn't as if there was any reason for him to decide that he wanted to be with her again, he just came in and out of her life at will -- that was his pattern. And in her mind, those drastic highs and lows felt like passion, instead of dysfunction.

When he would decide to call after days of silence,

she would feel the excitement building inside of her. All he had to do was say anything she wanted to hear -- and he knew everything that would pull her back in. When you are in that state of yearning for attention and affection, it doesn't even matter what you hear, as long as you hear *something*. And that, right there, is the thing: when you are overcome with a feeling of emptiness due to your partner's actions, that is never healthy. That is the definition of a low, or a valley. You want to hear anything to dispel the emptiness, because you yearn for another one of those peaks. You want to be thrust back into that addictive state of passion that makes you feel like you could be with that person forever. This is why you have to be careful not to mistake passion for love.

The constant desire for passion may allow you to overlook potentially good men. Passion can lie dormant in good men, undisturbed until the spark has been ignited. When you become accustomed to drama, the idea of someone who is easy to get along with can seem entirely undesirable -- boring. Years ago, while in the midst of a troubled, emotionally damaging relationship, I realized that instability would wreak havoc on my future. That cycle of passion would eventually prevent me from achieving my goals and overall success in my life. So, it wasn't easy, but I ended it. The overall vision and goals that

I had for my life outweighed my love for him. I chose me! Sometimes that is the realization you need. The most important thing is acknowledging the truth that leads you to make the hard decisions.

This is not something to feel badly about, or allow to negatively affect your feelings of self-worth. It can happen to everyone, and it most definitely happened to me. I missed out on exciting opportunities and countless experiences, because I was far too focused on my relationship drama. I remember my grandmother telling me that staying with certain types of men is like carrying a heavy sack of potatoes. You will either never reach your goals because the weight of the potatoes is too heavy, or when you finally reach your goal, you will be exhausted, run down, and unhappy. Grandmothers always give the best advice!

Since women tend to be more emotional than men, you sometimes misinterpret as passion the drastic highs and lows you experience with a man. They are not. When that passionate high is in full force, and he has you feeling on top of the world, he does all the right things and has made up for every mistake. Then, when the passion falls off again, you try to make excuses as to why the bad times are worth trudging through. The reality is that you just want so badly to feel what you felt during the high moments. And just like that, the cycle continues. These types of relationships tend to give men the upper hand, which is why you should be adamant about avoiding them.

When two people are truly compatible, there is no unhealthy cycle. No relationship is perfect. Sometimes it may seem like a healthy, stable relationship is uneventful, but that represents the laying of a stable foundation. Passion should come from stability in a healthy relationship, not a quality to build on. Like the parable of the man who builds his house on the shores of the sea, build your house on solid ground and it will last. Build your house on the sand, and it will be washed out to sea as soon as the waters get rough.

If any of this sounds familiar, don't worry. Now you're equipped with ways to prevent these mistakes moving forward. Go back to your list, and if you are tempted to begin something that you know, deep down, won't end well, take it off your list. On second thought, add it to your list of deal breakers. You can definitely have passion in your relationship, just let it grow from a healthy, stable relationship that doesn't cause you repeated heartache.

Changing your attractions also means looking for signs in men that show emotional, romantic, or mental unavailability. So, what exactly are those signs? Well, to be honest, some men are like wounded dogs limping from date to date with no true intention of making you someone special in their life. He may present himself as single and looking for a mature relationship, but in reality he is incapable of achieving what he claims to be in search of. It may not be his fault, and he may not mean to waste your time; but attempting to form a relationship really will prove to be a waste of time on both sides. Be on the lookout for the signs of emotionally and mentally unavailable men. The causes of unavailability can be wide-ranging; but probably the most common is being hurt by a woman from his past, beyond the point of recovery (at least at the present moment). This can be a warning signal. Overall, just trust your instincts -- most of the time, our instincts hold at least some kind of truth. Intuition is key!

Consider the analogy of the wounded dog. Wounded dogs have been hurt by someone in the past without doing anything to deserve the pain inflicted upon them. After being hurt, they carry with them a steel barrier around their metaphorical heart that protects them from being hurt again. They are defensive, not as friendly as they were before their wound, and their primary goal is to not get hurt again. Until they learn to trust others, they will not be able to truly develop a relationship with someone, for they will always be defending themselves. This is not the wounded dog's or the emotionally unavailable man's fault, necessarily, which is sad. But, it does not mean that you should be roped into something that will not provide you something equal in return.

What you need to make sure is that you avoid getting caught in the crossfire of a badly ended relationship. Even though men, who have been significantly hurt, are afraid of being hurt again, they also want to move past what has hurt them. That means they are highly likely to be looking for some kind of romance. And, as you have learned to this point, the man you are on a first date with does not always have similar goals in mind. It's important to be able to sniff out the symptoms of a badly wounded man, so that you don't walk away with a wound, as well.

Before you cancel all damaged men out, it is possible that just because a man has been hurt, even recently, he may still be ready to seek out something different. That is entirely his choice and recovery process. Your job is to find out more about his past break-up or painful experience, and let him explain it in the best way possible. Ask questions that determine his mindset at the present moment and his goals for future relationships. These types of questions will help you navigate the murky waters of a possibly still-damaged soul.

Habit Five Takeaways

- Change what you are attracted to at a foundational level and you will give yourself a better chance at finding love.
- Drastic ups and downs in a relationship can be detrimental to your personal growth and overall self-worth. Understand that healthy relationships are made with men who are reliable and consistent.
- Understand the difference between passion and compatibility. Compatibility leads to longevity and passion is derived from love, not instability.

Habit Five Reflections

1. Write down some qualities that you have been attracted to in the past that you recognize you need to change.

_____

_____

2. What are some actions you can take to help curb your attractions to the wrong men?

HABIT SIX: CHECK YOURSELF

Consider which part of the man you want to attract -- short term discipline for long term satisfaction.

If your ultimate goal is to be in a committed relationship that ultimately results in marriage, then it's in your interest to prevent yourself from becoming known as the fun girl, a woman who's easily available, or anything else that is negative or may be misrepresentative of your true character. So, what exactly does that mean? The fun girl is essentially a woman that a man calls for a good time. Does that necessarily mean sex? No, not always. But, what it does mean is that he may want to call you for drinks instead of dinner, perhaps closer to 10:00 p.m. instead of 7:00, then suggest that you accompany him to the club afterwards. These are not the actions of a man who has long term plans for you. You may also notice that he brings some friends along or asks you to bring friends. Group dates are not necessarily a negative thing. But, you have to be able to discern whether his goal is to introduce you to his friends, or a wild night of club hopping.

There are many simple ways to make sure you are not just viewed as the fun girl. The first thing you need to do is to present yourself as you want to be perceived. I know it may be hard to believe, but men categorize women. Just like we categorize men. You know after one date, within a few minutes of talking to someone, whether or not you can see yourself romantically involved with him, right? You also know within a few days whether or not you could see yourself being serious with someone, let alone marrying him. And, believe it or not, men subconsciously put you in a category based on how you present yourself.

What are the categories in this context? Nice, but not my type: *friend zone*. Alluring and sexy, but not relationship material: *fun girl*. Represents everything he ever wanted in a woman: *potential wife*. The categories may vary slightly for every man, but those are the basics. The great thing about this is that you can control how men perceive you, in most cases. There are some instances where a man may have issues with women. Maybe he has commitment issues or is just a dog, in which case you don't want to be part of that anyway. But, for the most part, men know quite early on whether they just want to sleep with you, or be potentially serious with you.

Let me pause for a second. Men are obviously very visual creatures. For most men, if you're beautiful or even remotely attractive, they will want to sleep with you -- it's just in their nature. It's your job to lead with much more restraint. You don't want to allow this to define you, and you most definitely don't want to get stuck in this category. Once you're known as the one to call for a wild night, it's nearly impossible to change that perception. Now, I'll explain the secrets to how you can ensure that you are not described as the fun girl. It may seem simple, but that doesn't stop many women from failing here. So, let's break it down so you know where to start:

Secret One: Present Yourself as the Ideal Woman

How you carry yourself is more than just how you

look. It relates to how you speak, the type of conversation you have, what your interests are, how you articulate your thoughts, and many other things. That doesn't mean you need a Harvard education to carry yourself well. You simply need to know how to talk about things that have value. I've heard too many times from men that they went on a date with a woman and she just talked non-stop about frivolous things. This can be a real turn off. Dive into what truly matters -- family, perhaps politics or the economy, travel, passions, creative exploits, and the like. If you are talking constantly about celebrity gossip, shopping, or other superficial things, you can come across as very worldly-minded.

Not only does this sort of conversation tell him that you may be a bit materialistic, it also translates that you don't really care about truly important topics. It prevents you from truly getting to know the core of someone. Remember, there are questions that we need to ask in order to discover a person's belief system, their morals and values. It's often said that you should never discuss religion or politics in the workplace. But when dating, all bets are off. You want to know how he feels about what's going on in the White House or how often he prays -- or if he ever prays.

Of course it is okay to lighten up the conversation

sometimes. There's absolutely nothing wrong with small talk. But, you also want to let him know that you are a smart, intelligent woman. Someone who cares about the direction of the world, as well as her career and life goals. So, when you are thinking about how to carry yourself, think simultaneously about what you truly care about. Think about what your interests are, your passions, your creative side. If you don't talk about things that matter, if you put more emphasis on what you are or aren't wearing, or if you walk by swinging your hips dramatically left to right, he may not take you seriously. Sure, these may be tactics that some women use, but not a woman who is serious about her future and focused on attracting a quality man to spend her life with.

Let me tell you a quick anecdote about two friends.

Kelly met Steve and instantly knew he couldn't meet her dating standards. Not only was he only working part-time, but he spent the rest of his time drinking and partying with his roommates. He checked off three deal breakers on her list -- ugh! But since she had been single for a year, she didn't see a problem dating him, just to pass the time. Steve was charming and knew how to show her a good time -- on a budget. Before she knew it, he'd worked his way into her bed, where he put on display his impressive skills -- overcompensation at its best. Big mistake! She followed that mind blowing sex down a rabbit hole for more than a year, only to come out empty-handed. She finally walked away realizing what she'd known since the very first date -- he wasn't someone she could build a relationship with.

Ladies, let me be clear: men who blow your mind in the bedroom are well aware of their abilities between the sheets, and they know just how to use that card. This is exactly why sex too early is a definite no! You want your mind clear, so you can focus on his character traits and identify red flags. I realize that you have needs, but think short-term discipline for long term satisfaction.

Secret Two: Subtly Demand Respect

I know the word 'demand' may seem forceful and angry. But it's actually just the opposite. See, I believe actions are what truly speaks for you, not words. Early on, you will have a conversation about what your expectations are. But eventually you will need to prove your words through actions, and expect proof of a man's words through his actions. This act is demanding respect, and you demand respect partly by respecting yourself first.

Here's the secret to allowing your actions to speak for you: when a man does something that you don't agree with, your initial response should be to pull back. For instance, if someone you've been dating suddenly stops calling -- don't call to cuss him out or send disgruntled text messages. And please, don't start sending subliminal messages with social media quotes. Sit back and wait. Once he calls you and acknowledges the severity of what has happened -- and notice I say *call* -- then you acknowledge him in return. If he texts you and says, "I haven't heard from you in a while," just say that you have been busy. The idea is that he calls to verbally initiate an apology or reconciliation. When he does so, expect clarity. Be clear with him but don't be nasty. Again, none of this is a job interview. He's not your employee and you're not reprimanding him. You're simply letting him know what your standard and expectation is for someone you are dating. Give him an opportunity to respond and an opportunity to make the correction. Ladies, you cannot expect a man to live up to a standard that you haven't made clear. Because all women have different standards, you cannot expect every man you date to know your standards up front.

The goal is to allow your standards to speak for

you, so make your expectations known. Not in a nasty or disgruntled way, but make them clear enough that he realizes he has two options: to meet your standards or move on. Standards lead to respect or release, remember? He will either learn from his mistake and make the correction or refuse. And if he refuses, then it's up to you to determine whether it qualifies as a deal breaker, or something that's worth giving more time.

Secret Three: Don't Lead with Sex

What does that mean? Well, I know you look at your TV screens and social media, and all you see is sex appeal. It is constantly glamorized. I know it seems like every man is looking for busting curves and low-cut tops. And maybe you think that if you don't look the part, then no man will be attracted to you. But that's not true. You have to consider which part of the man you are trying to attract. Aim to attract what is above the belt before appealing to what lies below the belt. He has already proven that he is drawn to your beauty, which is why he asked you out -- men are visual first, remember? Once you're on the date, your goal is to allow him to take notice of all the other amazing qualities you have to offer. This is when a man can begin to see you in a different way, because not every man is as shallow as they are portrayed. There will be plenty of time to explore the physical aspects of your chemistry as the relationship progresses. What you have to understand is this: if you rely on sex to attract a specific type of man, his attention will be fleeting. And since the goal is to be cherished for the long term, this is a huge mistake. Believe there is a man who is looking for someone just like you in your purest form. Have confidence in more than your body. And, don't feel for a second that men only want sex, because it is not the truth. If it is any consolation, look at the women who are wives, because that is the ultimate goal, right? You want to be taken seriously. You want to be the type of woman that a man can see himself marrying. I guarantee you that men who are looking for marriage aren't looking for the woman leaving nothing to the imagination.

The way you carry yourself can dictate how you feel throughout the day and ultimately the kind of day you have. If you walk confidently around the office as you work, you will be happy and confident. If you slouch on the couch, maybe you will become lazy and lack focus. Similarly, if you respect yourself, know your value, and place sex appeal on the backburner early on, a man will respect you enough to learn more about you. That is what you want. Most men would take sex if they feel it is being offered. And, the problem with that is if you give in to sex too soon, that also sets a standard. Most likely, he will lose interest in learning more about you even if you continue to try. First impressions are of the utmost importance. Don't allow yourself to fall into this trap -- getting too physical too early. Doing so goes against all the gems I'm offering in this book. Men only cherish women that require effort to pursue and acquire.

Habit Six Takeaways

- Once you are known as the *fun girl*, you will have a hard time changing the way you are perceived and treated.
- Just because men are visual doesn't mean you should lead with sex appeal. You have much more value to offer than sex. Giving a man sex too early can affect your ability to detect deal breakers.
- Men are attracted to women with goals and a good sense of independence. When you become serious with a man, be careful not to lose yourself.

Habit Six Reflections

1. Have you ever been on a first date with a guy that you really liked, but for some reason never heard from him afterwards? Looking back, is there anything you would have done differently?

_____
_____
_____
_____
_____
_____
_____
_____

2. Take an honest assessment of how you carry yourself while on a date? Can you think of some changes you can make to better present yourself?

_____
_____

JANTAE RASHAUN

PART TWO: GET OUT THERE

HABIT SEVEN: DATE WITH PURPOSE

Don't wait four or five dates down the road to find out he doesn't want a relationship.

What is the primary reason that dating relationships fail? Well, let's start with the definition of failure. Failure is not achieving the purpose of some venture. Anything without a clearly defined and specific purpose is indeed bound for failure. In other words, dating without purpose can set you up for failure. There must be a specific goal or intention involved to achieve a desired purpose.

How do you define purpose when you date? Act with purpose. Make purposeful conversation. Learn the important details about the person sitting across the table from you. Ask him meaningful questions.

Humor is great, and small talk is a nice segue into deeper conversation. Defining purpose at the beginning can be as straight-forward as simply getting to know a person, finding out what he is looking for at the present moment, and discovering how like-minded or different you are. The more you know about a person, the better you can decide whether to continue getting to know him, or whether your time could be spent better elsewhere. Dating just to date will produce just that: more dating with different men, or continuously dating the same guy because you just can't separate yourself from him. Defining each other's purpose is a great way to put standards in place and get to know one another's perspective.

There is no better time to truly get to know each other than on the first date. Why wait? Your time is valuable, and the time you spend with others is vital. Try to find out as soon as possible everything you have in common with the man you are spending time with. Identify the possible red flags. When you treat dating in a serious manner, you will find out what is attractive and what is a deal-breaker in a possible relationship. You will learn about yourself and others and eliminate wasted time. Find out about past relationships and why they failed, if you or the other person is comfortable with sharing those details. Be forward with parts of your own dating history and your expectations. Think about it this way: these questions will be nearly impossible to shy away from as the dating phase progresses, so why not get them out of the way as soon as possible? If there are red flags, you will find out before moving any further. If you are both of the same mindset, you will be more confident and assured if you decide to continue dating and learning about each other.

Not only does dating with a purpose guarantee that you will not waste your time on someone who doesn't match up to your expectations, it simplifies the dating process and prioritizes your valuable time. It's perfectly fine to start dating because you enjoy someone's company. However, women must have the wherewithal to know when to ask the real questions. This example can be a touchy subject to bring up. "So, I wanted to ask -- are you dating anyone else? Are you looking for anything serious, right now?" Those are just some of the dreaded, yet necessary questions. Sometimes, questions like these will stop a man in his tracks. But, does that mean the date is a failure? No. That simply means that you have enough self-worth to inquire about his intentions early on. Why wait until four or five dates down the road to learn that he's not in the market for a relationship. Your time is valuable.

This doesn't mean that you have to treat these

questions like an interrogation, or like you are on higher ground than him. You are on a date with him for a reason. Be understanding -- he doesn't owe you anything, just like you don't owe him anything. That's why the first date is such an ideal and practical setting to get these hard questions out of the way. If a man admits to infidelity in past relationships, you may feel less entitled to overreact. There are actually positive ways of looking at this situation. If a man admits to certain things on the first date, it may mean that he is taking his date with you seriously. He is being upfront and honest. Either way, this is something you would want to know, without a doubt, sooner rather than later.

You see, most men go through different phases in their lives, especially in their truly developmental years -- not puberty or adolescence, but in their twenties. Young men often go through a wild phase of infidelity. It's another biological fact that men mature much later than women. This is true throughout the first stages of life, from childhood to early adulthood. Often, experience can be the best teacher. The point is this: if a man hypothetically comes clean to you about infidelity in past relationships, this could be a sign that he has grown from that experience. This may not always be the case, but many times it is. We have all made mistakes, and it is no one's place to judge these mistakes, except when they concern your own well-being. So, make the best judgment for yourself. What you learn may be a red flag, or you may feel comforted by his honesty.

In addition to defining purpose with the man you are interested in dating -- you must also ask *yourself* key questions such as, "Can this develop into something long-term?" Asking yourself this question is not the same as asking yourself, "Do I want to marry this person right now?" It is simply considering whether you could see what he brings to the table developing into the type of relationship that has longevity. This is laying the foundation of a purpose. Purpose grows more tangible as the relationship develops past the pursuit phase, and into the acquired and exclusive phase.

Dating with a purpose builds on the foundation of this book. Once you have clearly defined your standards, desired qualities, and deal breakers, you will know your purpose with dating down to the specifics. On a larger scale, you will know you want a man who pursues you with intentions to acquire you, so that he will cherish you long term. On a smaller scale, regarding the specific qualities of the man as an individual, you must focus on your personal standards, expectations, and desires. Define your larger purpose to match your standards and you will be ready to date with a goal in mind: to attract the man of your dreams.

Habit Seven Takeaways

- Dating with purpose starts with building the right standards and identifying desired qualities and deal breakers.
- Understanding your purpose of dating is essential to determining whether a man is worth your time and energy.
- Once you realize your dating purpose, it is essential to ask men the right questions.

Habit Seven Reflections

1. Can you recall an instance when you negated to ask the right questions on a date? What lessons did you learn from that situation?

_____
_____
_____
_____

2. Based on that lesson, what is the most important question you will ask on your future dates?

HABIT EIGHT: DECODE HIS INTENTIONS

Your true value stretches far beyond your body.

Just as shifting your mindset is foundational to developing a relationship that succeeds, knowing where you stand with a man keeps you from wasting your time. Knowing what you mean to him, and indeed, knowing his intentions, allows you to decipher his goals for the relationship. Men can be complicated creatures. It may be hard to figure out what they want, or what actually attracts them. Figuring this out, as well, can be complicated or quite direct, depending on the man.

Believe it or not, men are not only drawn to beauty. They don't just decide a woman is attractive and want to date her. Men are just as complicated as women, despite what they would have you think, ladies. Thanks to social media and online dating, they have more options than ever -- whether they are looking for a good time, a long-term relationship, or just someone to pass the time. But, with so many options at their fingertips, men are now dating with a purpose -- but not quite the same way as women. Admittedly, they are typically not as focused and intentional as women are, but they know in the early stages the role they envision playing in your life. Figuring out what that is, and the thought process they are going through, is another story, though. Understanding a man's thought process could be as easy as hearing it directly from him; or it could be more difficult, requiring deeper digging and persistent questioning. Note that if a man is turned off by your questions, then you know where you stand -- and maybe that is a good reason to focus your attention elsewhere.

As women, we are typically pursued by a man, not the other way around. This was one of the first topics I discussed. Despite the rise in encouragement of pursuit by women, if you focus on being pursued, then you will be. Therefore, it is extremely important to attract who you want to be pursued by. Who you attract is nearly as important as who you are attracted to, because it determines the men you date

-- and, eventually, marry. Like it or not, men are always drawn to the physical first -- they are visual by nature. So, let's break down what will attract each specific type of man, in a broad sense. First of all, there are three main reasons that men date.

The first reason men date is to have a good time, in other words, satisfy their physical needs. Avoid dating men in this phase, especially if you are in the market for something meaningful and real. This type of man is typically guarded, so please don't attempt to use your body to win him over -- you'll just set yourself up to be hurt and extremely disappointed. If a man tells you that he is only looking for a "friends with benefits" situation -- believe him! This type of honesty is not some sort of game to get you into bed. It's likely a blatant truth that is intended to prevent you envisioning him as Mr. Right. The clearest message that he's looking to be nothing more than Mr. Right Now. Dating a man who is only looking for a physical connection is a waste of your time; your value stretches far beyond your body. Obviously, this type of man is not one that should be entertained. Your self-worth should never be devalued, and your body is no exception. But, if you have found yourself unknowingly attracted to this type of man, that means you are... human. Don't read too far into it, unless you are noticeably displaying a substantial amount of cleavage or a dress so short that you are sending the wrong message -- you may want to make some changes. This type of guy may not always be upfront about his true intentions, but if you pay close attention, trust, the signs are there. Does he check off any qualities from the list below?

Signs He's Here for Sex

- ☐ Only wants to see you during late hours
- ☐ Says he's not looking for a relationship
- ☐ Never takes you out in public
- ☐ Suggests "friends with benefits"
- ☐ Disappears for days inbetween sex
- ☐ Claims monogamy is unnatural
- ☐ Refuses to put a title on your "situation"

Ladies, don't be afraid to ask questions if you are uncertain of a man's purpose for you -- and make sure his actions align with his responses. If he skirts the questions or dances around the answers, that just may

DATING STANDARDS THAT SPEAK

be your answer. Once the writing is on the wall, let that be the last opportunity he gets to waste your time!

The second reason men date is to simply see where things can go, without a specific goal in mind. There's nothing inherently wrong with this, as we all have been there. On a positive note, this is likely a sign that he is in a comfortable phase in his life and capable of acquiring and committing to the *right* woman. These dates happen when a man finds you attractive with qualities potentially fit for him long-term. However, don't get too excited yet -- he can be swayed in one direction or the other solely based on the way you carry yourself. This is not a deal breaker, by any means, but it is imperative that you shift your mindset and allow your standards to speak to each of your astonishing qualities. Set yourself apart. I'm not suggesting that you pander to his tastes, or even that you can. Just be your authentic, amazing self, and he will take notice.

The final reason men date is if they are looking for someone special to be part of their life -- a potential wife. Hopefully, this reason is also your purpose for dating. Knowing the man you are dating has good intentions that are backed up with actions, will ensure that you are both on the same page. This is the type you truly want to attract. If a man is well aware of what he wants, consistent in his actions, and prepared to commit to the right woman, it suggests that he has encountered life-changing experiences that have resulted in his readiness for something good and true. The scripture says it best in Proverbs 18:22, which reads *"He who finds a wife finds a good thing and obtains favor from the Lord."* If you have drawn interest from this type of man, it doesn't guarantee that marriage is on the horizon -- but you are on the right path. Attracting a mature man who is prepared to acquire and cherish you speaks something about you, as well. It's a sure sign that you have successfully learned to apply each of the dating habits in this book to your daily life. Yes!

Watch For Red Flags

Knowing how to spot red flags is a big part of decoding a man's intentions. Now that you're clear on your deal breakers, red flags should be much easier to identify. Let's face it, men aren't always honest and up front about who they are and what they *really* want from you. This is why it's crucial to know exactly how to sniff out signs that can lead you to hidden truths. The major difference between deal breakers and red flags is that deal breakers are often solid, tangible facts that can't be ignored. For instance, if you want kids and a guy tells you that he never wants them -- it's a definite reason to walk away, a deal breaker. Remember, you are only choosing to date men who measure up to your standards and what you truly want out of life. Red flags, on the other hand, aren't necessarily as easy to notice. They give you a sneak peak into some truths that someone may be hiding behind words or calculated actions.

Red flags are any sign that may be indicative of a greater issue. They can take many forms, and that is what I will touch on in this section. They are different for everyone, but many are constant across relationships. For instance, relationship issues in the past may be a red flag for everyone, regardless of whether they end up being deal breakers or not. And regardless of whether they are deal breakers, they should not be overlooked. If they are neglected, they grow in size until they are impossible to ignore. If they are confronted, they may be easily explained -- you don't want a red flag to morph into a deal breaker if it can be resolved early on.

Everyone does, in fact, have different red flags. Therefore, you should rely on your intuition. If something seems like a red flag to you, then it probably is. The bottom line is that you must not ignore anything that seems like it could develop into a major challenge in your relationship. This habit is fairly straightforward, and should be. An analysis of red flags should be concise and to the point, because it is highly important to notice them and know what to do about them. There are some red flags that are deal breakers, and some that may just need to be addressed. I have touched on a few red flags already, but it's important to know there are two general areas of red flags: red flags that stem from past experience, or red flags that arise through action in your relationship with him.

In the first area, the best way to find out about his past is through conversation. You can definitely ask about his past relationships, as stated in previous chapters. But learning about more serious past struggles in his life like childhood issues, addiction, or even depression, can take time to uncover. These are things that can be explained, and may, in fact, provide evidence of his true character. I have a close friend who is a former alcoholic, and has been clean for five years. He is better for it. I would consider him one of the strongest people I know. However, in dating, sometimes past issues like this can be a red flag, because they may be things that would make you want to avoid further commitment. You don't want to be hurt down the road because of something you didn't know about him, or something that could have been avoided had you known about it.

In the second area, you need to be more aware. Pay attention constantly to the way he acts, and if he is shady about where he is going at night, or something similar, this may be a red flag. Even if it's harmless, it does not deserve to be ignored. You should still acknowledge it and ask for an explanation. In fact, lack of or insufficient explanation for something that may worry you is one of the biggest indicators. It means that he is either being dishonest, or doesn't care enough about your feelings to convince you otherwise. Trust is one of the most vital elements in a relationship. Without trust even a healthy, happy relationship cannot survive. Proverbs 25:19 reminds us that *"Confidence in an unfaithful man in time of trouble is like a bad tooth and a foot out of joint."*

Ignoring our intuition is refusing to read between the lines. Actions always take precedence over words. The only way you can diagnose a red flag is by asking about his intentions, observing his actions, and following your own standards. You also have to let him know your standards. If he doesn't know them, he may break them without realizing. Again, in diagnosing red flags, you have to use your womanly intuition. If something is too worrisome to get past, then it's not worth further stressing over. Back out of the relationship before it progresses any further, because that red flag will never disappear -- it will always be there, and only grow, looming over your relationship like a constant stressor in the back of your mind.

Again, no matter what the red flag is, don't ignore it. This, too, will loom over a relationship. The only way you can address a red flag and resolve it is to confront him or leave the relationship. Doing nothing about it will only cause you pain. It is only fair to him and to yourself to address it as soon as doubt arises in your mind. It's also important to remember that although a red flag may not be his fault, it doesn't have to be accepted. There are two members of every relationship, and although it may not be fun for him, it is your choice what to accept and what to refuse in your relationship. You deserve the best.

Habit Eight Reflections

1. Think about someone you are currently dating or dated recently. What do his actions say about his intentions with you?

_____
_____
_____
_____

DATING STANDARDS THAT SPEAK

_____
_____
_____
_____

2. Write down the clear signs that he has shown to give you insight into his intentions.

_____
_____
_____
_____
_____
_____
_____
_____

HABIT NINE: DECODE HIS DATE

Have standards for the types of dates you accept -- no more dating just to date.

Knowing the perspective from which a man approaches a date is vital to understanding his true intentions. The ability to decode his date right away will help you decide whether he intends to take you seriously. You can actually start evaluating his intentions before the date has even begun and prepare yourself for what is to come. Here are a few points you might consider before the first date:

1. How soon did he secure your time? When he asked you out, how far in advance did he call? Was it a week prior? Two days

before? Or worse, did he text a few hours before he wanted to meet saying, "Hey, what are you up to tonight? Do you want to meet me at this spot?" This is a sure sign that you were part of his last-minute plans. It also tells you that maybe his previous plans fell through suddenly. Sure, maybe he was sitting at home, bored, and searching for something to do. Either way, do not accept this. You do not deserve to be the "just something to do" girl. This is not how you want to be considered, and this is not how a man who is taking you seriously will approach you.

2. And, this is extremely important, you want to be on the lookout for the type of date he proposes. Not all dates are created equally. Let's break down the three main types of dates and what they represent.

Type One: The Swipe Date

The first type of date is the swipe date. The reason I call it a swipe date is because of the modern era online dating and the social media craze. Just as quickly as you can swipe, you can set up a date with your "match" on just about any dating app that exists. Not only have neither of you truly given any thought to what kind of date you would like to go on, but you have also not had a chance to learn whether or not you are compatible.

The worst aspect of online dating is that it matches you at the most simplified level with an abundance of people chosen by the most basic characteristics. Do some people have success with online dating? I'm sure they do. But generally, I find that even people who use dating apps eventually feel it's a waste of their time. This is what I'm hearing from single women, so imagine how the single men feel. One thing you have to consider is that typically the man pays for the date, right? So, if he is matching with hundreds of people, he is just scanning the field to find out who he could possibly date. He has matched up with so many people that dating becomes a monthly bill of some sort. I truly believe that this is one of the reasons that men don't take women on many traditional dates anymore, and also why men expect women to step up and pay as early as the first date.

So where do you go for a swipe date? Well, you may meet at the bar or at a local restaurant for appetizers and a drink -- someplace close, somewhere you can walk to depending on where you live. So, basically, a swipe date is something that is not a huge investment monetarily or timewise. As I mentioned earlier, he may also expect you to pay for either half, or maybe even all, of the bill. He may also cut the date short. I have heard far too many horror stories from online dating. Take Ava for example:

Ava was matched with Ellis on her favorite dating app. where he checked off several of the ideal qualities she wanted in a man. After texting each other for a few days, he invited her to meet him for an afternoon at the beach the following day. He seemed sweet and the thought of a romantic walk on the beach gave her a good feeling about him. When she arrived, she was shocked to see that he was at least five inches shorter than he claimed in his online profile. Really? On top of that, he was already soaked and sweaty from swimming in the ocean -- still she gave him a chance. As they walked and talked, somewhere between the evasive responses to her questions and his wandering eyes, he fixated on the fact that she was wearing a dress over her bikini. Then, he had the nerve to suggest that she rub sunblock all over him so he wouldn't burn. Just when she thought things couldn't get any worse, he changed his demeanor and asked if she wanted to grab lunch. She thought they were headed towards one of the restaurants on the pier -- no such luck. He stopped at the nearby taco truck, placed his order, then told her that he left his wallet in the car! That was her LAST swipe date.

What have you learned from this? If anything, it's that he didn't invest any time, effort, or money into the date. If you invest time into someone, you expect him to do the same. The problem with the swipe date, and online dating in general, is the lack of initial investment required. And too often, minimal investment paired with an endless number of options at your fingertips leads to a lack of overall effort. The same type of nonsense that Ava encountered with Ellis. Not all online dates are disastrous, but be weary of the swipe date, because it succeeds far less than a traditional date.

Type Two: The Left Side of the Menu Date
This is the date with someone who probably doesn't mind spending a lot of money. Which may sound good, but are you just an object to him? Your Left Side of the Menu man may not be rich, but he is most likely well-off. The kind of guy that believes that money *can* buy love -- or at least affection. He is going to show up in his expensive car, take you to the best restaurants, and speak about the lavish life. His

goal is to convince you that money is no object, and that he spent a substantial amount of time and effort planning your date. At the same time, he is well aware that you are looking at the left side of the menu -- the expensive side, the side that comes with strings attached. You have to be careful here, because someone like this has intentions that can be hard to uncover. Is he overcompensating for something? Does he just want to get you into bed, or worse, does he expect that on the first date? There is absolutely nothing wrong with a man taking the time to wine and dine you -- if his purpose is merely to make you feel special. The best thing to do in this situation is to show him that at the core of your standards is self-worth -- and money is not enough to compromise your values.

Type Three: The Traditional Date

This type of date occurs when a man asks you out in advance to meet for a traditional first date. Most of the time he asks for a date around a week in advance. Coffee, dinner, a movie, a walk in the park, or something similar are perfectly acceptable for a first date. The reason they are acceptable for dates is because they have been PLANNED in advance and meet the primary qualifications for a good date (that will more than likely satisfy what a date is meant to achieve). These are perfect for talking, making eye-contact, and getting to know one another. There is no pressure caused by time or the question of sleeping with one another, because if a man has asked you on a date like this, he is likely serious about his interest in you. You want to be able to look in his eyes, not because you will "fall in love" or develop some sort of wild sexual attraction for each other, but because a person's eyes tell you a lot about his intentions, personality, and thought process. Being able to sit down and look into your date's eyes is extremely important.

Now, let's take a look at examples of the types of questions you should ask on the traditional date.

Number One: Are you originally from this area? If not, where are you from?

This may seem like a strange question to ask right off the bat. However, the reason you ask this question so early is because it opens the door to finding out more about his history or background without being too invasive. So, for instance, if he says, "Oh no, I'm not from here, I'm originally from Louisiana. I came up here for college and I stayed." You respond with, "Really? Wow, okay! So you're from the south. What college did you attend up here?" Which, of course, also leads to questions about what he studied, if he played sports, or if he was a member of any clubs or organizations. Then, you can offer a little bit about yourself. Afterwards you can move on to the juicier things you would like to know, once you have established a good rapport.

Number Two: Are you currently seeing anyone seriously?

This is a question that's going to require some thought, because men are masters at avoiding questions like this. Your date might say, "Oh no, I'm not dating anybody seriously," when in reality he may have been seeing someone on and off for months. While he may not consider his relationship serious, the other girl may indeed consider it serious, and your date might not want to mention it. So, this is a question you will need to follow up or clarify. If he answers no, then you might ask, "Okay, so when was your last relationship?"

Keep following up, no matter whether he says his last relationship was two years ago or two months ago. You might then ask, "Why did that end?" Do you see how these are the makings of productive and interesting conversation? No, I'm not saying you should question your date by sitting him down like you're in a job interview, and just start spewing all these questions. You're going to go through small talk about what you like to do in your free time and what you do for a living. However, you surely want to have the important conversations early on. Why? Because you are busy, and you do not want to waste your time on something that will not be positive for you. You want to know what you are getting yourself into as soon as possible because your time is valuable and irreplaceable.

Number Three: Get a little deeper.

You want to dig deeper early on because everyone has different standards. One example concerns dating men with children. Some women have children of their own, whereas other women don't want to date a man with children at all. Everyone is different. So, again, dig deep early -- learn the information that you deem important. Come with a follow-up question and a follow-up reply, no matter the answer. For most women the deal breaker is that their date has children, not that he doesn't; so don't make him feel bad if he says he's a father (even if it is a deal breaker). If he says he does have children, then ask how many, and if they are all by the same mother. By the end of the first date, you should have these questions answered. He will either be talking, or relatively quiet, but no matter his responses, you will have gained enough information to know whether this is something you want to continue or put an end to. Of course, you don't need to ask these questions one after another like it's a police interrogation. But knowing this information will avoid wasting everyone's time.

It may seem glaringly obvious that a traditional date should be the goal -- but still, somehow, find yourself out on a dead-end date. Give yourself a break. Times have changed and more and more women are allowing loneliness to push them into lowering their standards. This is a short term solution that ultimately ruins your chances of attracting the man who will cherish you. And, of course, that is the goal. Don't allow the need for companionship to cause you to settle.

Quantity Doesn't Equal Quality

There is no word to describe how much the dating game has changed in the past ten years with the onset of social media and various forms of online dating. Whether it's the endless scrolling through your daily timeline, or swiping left and right past hundreds of lackluster dating profiles on your favorite dating app, quantity seems to be taking a hold over quality in our dating culture. All of this "quantity" has distracted us from making wise choices when investing our time into men. This issue is especially prevalent in the realm of dating. And while it is extremely common to find available members of the opposite sex this way, the foundation of a vast majority of successful relationships is set through a real-life first encounter. There's no substitution for quality, and the replacement is most definitely not quantity.

Disconnecting from the internet and social media culture that permeates our society at every level can be extremely difficult. There's no disputing this. No matter who you are, it's likely that you have been faced with the thought that you should re-evaluate some aspect of your life based on the facades portrayed all too often on social media. Online dating and social media in today's culture is just one example of the disparity between quality and quantity.

I've spoken to many women who have grown so frustrated with dating that they have resorted to dating apps, which, by design, will definitely present plenty of options. But quantity does not equal quality! Sure, there are success stories, but they are very few and far between. It can be difficult to avoid settling for easy ways to meet men when you are constantly tempted by guys who turn out to be nothing more than shirtless profile photos and not-so-witty one-liners. Getting back to the basics of dating, though, can be the simplest way of returning to a quality-based dating scene. Simply shunning social media direct messages and online dating might not work as a sole remedy. These options have to be replaced with higher quality alternatives. A huge part of that is knowing where to go to be in the company of the type of man you want to attract.

Go to places and events where you can interact with like-minded, high-quality men. Period. That doesn't mean to be dishonest or insincere about who you are and your choice pastimes, just to find quality men. You can meet a man just about anywhere. The idea is to connect at places that aline with your true interests. This definitely increases the chances that he will align with your standards. Again, you want to become your expectations, and doing so can inadvertently put you in the best places to meet good men. Use the list below as a starting point to identifying the best places for you to meet men.

Quality Places to Meet Men

- ☐ *Workplace*
- ☐ *Bookstore*
- ☐ *Charity Event*
- ☐ *Gym*
- ☐ *Networking Event*
- ☐ *Grocery Store*
- ☐ *Sporting Event*
- ☐ *Volunteer Program*

Online dating has had a very negative impact on more traditional ways of meeting potential dates -- especially for men. Since studies show that women outnumber men in the world, some men can be tricked into believing their opportunities are endless. Additionally, with such a wide range of dating options, many men are putting less time, effort, and energy into the women they date. Hundreds of pretty faces waiting to match is too much temptation for even the humblest of men to handle. The result, of course, is often last-minute, poorly planned, quick-fix dates. This approach to dating contradicts every habit I have laid out throughout this book. The idea is for men to pursue, earn or acquire you, right? For a woman to accept this blatant absence of effort from a potential partner is completely out of the question. You are worth more than just a bunch of meaningless dates with men who are checking names off of a list. You deserve quality. The company you keep, even in dating, reflects upon you. Quality over quantity is just as much about personal self-worth as self-respect. Seek quality in men and you will attract quality.

Habit Nine Takeaways

- With social media and the internet, there is more quantity in the dating arena than ever before, but this doesn't necessarily lead to quality.
- Take the time to make a list of ideal places that you can meet men with similar interests.

Habit Nine Reflections

1. Can you recall the worst date you've ever been on? Explain the factors that made it so terrible.

___

2. Just as you need clarity on the vision for your life and ideal man, it's important to know your expectations for a date. Describe your ideal date.

___

HABIT TEN: DON'T LOSE YOURSELF

Never sacrifice yourself for the sake of having a man.

Once you have been successfully pursued by a man who meets your needs and desires, he will soon be prepared to take things to the next level and acquire your love. And when you are in an exclusive relationship, many aspects will change; yet, some will remain the same. Part of maintaining the dating dynamic between men and women is to remain elusive throughout the relationship. In other words, don't lose your identity in love. The idea is that your man should not become too comfortable, which breeds complacency. Complacency, of course, leads to mistakes. Aside from this reality, part of what makes us attractive as women (not only physically, but mentally and emotionally) is being elusive, or hard to catch -- because you are booked and busy. Additionally, if you are hard to catch, a man who loves you, who is set on fully acquiring you, will not let up in his pursuit. This is exactly what you want. What does being elusive mean? At its core, elusiveness describes who you are and how you carry yourself. You have to be assured, clever, and independent enough for a man to realize that you are not desperate for love -- you are happy, fulfilled and open to the *right* man.

Men are attracted to women who are smart, attractive, and confident. They want women who possess a strong sense of independence, women with goals they are working toward achieving, other than just finding a husband. The harder and longer you search for love, the less likely you are to find it. So, whether it's that next big promotion at work, finishing your degree, or saving for your first home, you should focus on something that keeps you motivated each day. This is more than advice for love, it is advice for life. Once you become involved with a man, you must strive to ensure the drive toward your accomplishments remains strong. In fact, your drive should grow stronger than ever. Be careful not to lose yourself in a man.

Part of being elusive is knowing how important it is to learn to keep your relationship separate from the aspects of your life that require extreme focus. This advice doesn't suggest that the man in your life shouldn't be aware of the important aspects in your life. It's a wonderful thing to be able to share dreams and future goals with him. But, you must know how to balance love and work. Love often tips the scale in its own favor, which can be detrimental to other aspects of our personal lives.

A man should never come before family, business, or any of your future goals, unless he is your husband. For example, do not miss work or school just to spend time with him. If he feels as if you would drop anything just to be with him, what does he have left to work towards? Be responsible. No one wants to date a person who loses sight of her goals and aspirations so easily. It's a sign of immaturity. Besides, there are plenty of ways to squeeze him into your thriving, busy life. Instead of skipping out on commitments and prior engagements, arrange time together before or after, even if it's a thirty-minute coffee date or walk in the park. Find ways to show that you are interested, but remain elusive and focused on other goals in your life. The trick is to make your time together quality, regardless of the quantity. The secret is to keep him wanting more.

As women, we tend to throw ourselves fully into our relationships. Then, we end up losing ourselves if things don't lead down the aisle. That's why it's so crucial that you maintain your personal life throughout your journey to find lasting love. When you are at work or school, you should focus on your goals, not on constantly calling or texting him. It's perfectly fine to take a few minutes to talk to him during one of your breaks. Just don't allow your conversation to delve into anything that will cause you to be consumed by relationship matters throughout the remainder of the day.

This especially applies when you and your significant other are going through a rough patch and you're feeling less secure about the relationship. Every relationship experiences hard times, but if you find that you can't function normally during the lows, you may need to reconsider your mental, physical, and emotional attachment to him. The idea is to guard your heart and be wise about who you allow to tap into your emotions. This is a problem that many women encounter time and time again. You want to trust your heart to a man whom you can be certain will respect it and handle it with care. Choose someone who allows you to be focused and successful while maintaining a healthy love life. Relationships are work, but the work shouldn't be so overwhelming that it intrudes on your productivity in other aspects of your life.

Balance Love and Life

There are some very important things to understand and put into play once you are seriously dating someone -- matters particularly pertaining to your career, family, and social life. As women, we often make the mistake of incorporating our man too heavily and too quickly into our lives. Many of us tend to include him in every aspect of our lives only because we have begun exclusively dating. What you have to understand, though, is that your life remains *your* life until you have been fully acquired. That understanding is the ultimate goal.

The only way the man will fully understand the goal is if the right boundaries are in place. He has to feel as if he is still working towards something. The battle has not been won. The gift has not been opened. Let me paint a picture for you. Once you have your career, whether you own a business, work for a company, or teach at a school, you have fought hard to maintain a healthy work-life balance, right? So, once you intertwine your significant other into that established balance, it takes a bit of a shift. However, the shift doesn't occur the way you are thinking -- your work-life balance morphs into a work-life-*love* balance. Read that carefully. Love becomes its own separate entity, apart from work and life. This balance is the secret to maintaining your current life course, dreams, goals, and responsibilities -- without losing yourself too early in a relationship.

In addition to your career and family, your social life is extremely important. The years of investment in relationships with girlfriends or social groups are valuable, and shouldn't take a back seat to a new man in your life. Every type of relationship plays an important role in our lives. After all, your friends are the ones you'll call on to pick up the pieces if things don't work out in the long run. So, once you decide to incorporate a man into your life, carve out a separate space for him. The secret is to maintain your constant sense of self that you had before he came along. It's much easier to move on from a failed relationship if you have maintained a strong sense of self throughout the experience. Let me tell you a story about Alicia, who was infamous for falling hard and fast for men.

Alicia fell for a particular guy and let everything else in her life fall by the wayside. She stopped pushing for her goals, left her favorite dance class, and started regularly skipping her weekly dinners with her best friends. She spent every free minute with her new guy for the better part of six months. Once things started spiraling downward, though, he began to entertain thoughts of other women. Soon, his thoughts turned into cheating. Alicia became deeply disturbed at the thought of losing him to someone else. She stayed with him as long as she could, through every up and down, but just became more and more depressed. One day, he finally walked away and left her for another woman. Through her rough patch, she had missed so much work that her career suffered. Alicia had lost touch with her former support system, so she struggled alone. Months later, she finally fully recovered, realizing how much time she had wasted. It was time to rebuild.

Now, this may sound like a drastic situation, but it happens more than you realize. The lesson, though, is this -- you should always, always maintain your identity when you are with a man. Never sacrifice yourself for the sake of having a man. Otherwise, it can be hard for you to imagine your life without him. The bottom line is that you need to maintain a healthy balance between love and all other areas of life. But how do you pull this off and still build a relationship?

Plan your time with him according to your work schedule. That means that if you know you have to get up for work the next day, don't be out with him all night -- save that for the weekends. Leave time for yourself, too, and block off time for family and friends in the meantime. Remember, you're not only presenting yourself at your job and cultivating other important bonds, you're also sending a message to him. You don't want to give the illusion that you're willing to drop things that are important just for him -- at least not at this phase.

At this point, you have not been fully acquired. So, that means he hasn't earned the time you spend at work making progress in your career, or at school getting an education. It also doesn't mean that he should take the place of your creative pursuits. Be strong and willing to set aside the phone, plan your days out, and tell him that you will not be available at certain times. Do this immediately, because if you give him the idea that you are always available for him, it will form a habit and be harder to break once you realize you have been sacrificing highly important areas of your life for him.

Those evening hours you spend writing in your journal, attending a dance class, or grabbing dinner with your friends are valuable and should not be easily exchanged. Everything that makes you undeniably who you are needs to be kept in place at all costs. If he can't understand that, it probably means that he doesn't truly appreciate who you are in the first place. He has to work to gain access to your time, which will make him want to acquire it.

Once you have adopted the proper mindset for dating, keeping a healthy work-life-love balance will be easy. You will only have to worry about the practicalities. Just remember, ladies, that no man is worth sacrificing your time until you are fully acquired -- and even then, don't fail to maintain your strong and unwavering sense of identity.

Habit Ten Takeaways

- Being elusive is one of the major keys to maintaining a position of pursuit in a relationship. The secret is to keep him wanting more of you.
- Never allow a man to negatively infringe on other important areas of your life.
- Important relationships in your life should not immediately take a backseat to a new man in your life.

Habit Ten Reflections

1. Have you ever experienced a break up that had a negative impact on your career or social life? Looking back, how would you change things?

_____
_____
_____
_____
_____
_____
_____
_____

2. When was the last time you dropped everything to make time for a man? Do you think it had a positive effect to how things progressed between the two of you?

_____
_____

FINAL WORDS

Nowadays, attracting a man who protects, comforts, motivates, and understands you, often seems a daunting task. We have all been disappointed by past relationships, of course, but finding the man of your dreams is more realistic and attainable than it may seem. Hopefully, *Dating Standards That Speak* makes it crystal clear that you can control the narrative in so many ways, but it takes a good amount of self work to do so. Anything that you desire to change in your life requires faith and effort, which we know from James 2:17 *"Even so faith, if it does not have works, is dead in itself."*

Each and every one of you should realize your self-worth. Believing that you should be sought after doesn't mean you shouldn't be rocking the world with

FINAL WORDS

your feminine power. In fact, it acknowledges that feminine power. You have to change your mindset to acknowledge your true standards, and follow it up with dating habits that demonstrate self-respect. We all want to find love, but are you willing to do the inner work to change your innate responses to men? That means never settling for anyone who doesn't meet your expectations and treat you according to your value. That means preparing yourself to entertain *only* the men who meet the standards you have established to reflect the overall vision for your life.

Adopting the habits in this book does not guarantee you will immediately find the man you will spend your life with, but it does give you a solid blueprint for successful dating. Only when you acknowledge your own value and stop settling for less, will you attract men who are willing to earn your affection and love you long term. Only when you realize that *you* are the prize will you be sought after as such. Every shift that you make to your mindset and actions has a mirror image. When you treat yourself with respect, when you have standards for every man you allow into your life, and when you know your role in this world -- happiness and love will find you.

The right man for you is out there, the one who wants to love, cherish, and commit to you. All you have to do is prepare yourself to be found. My prayer is that the principles in this book leave you with the understanding that once you put the *right* standards in place -- they truly speak volumes. As you step back into the dating world with a new found confidence, I wish you nothing but love and fulfillment. You deserve it.

Many blessings,

Jantae

www.ingramcontent.com/pod-product-compliance
Lightning Source LLC
Chambersburg PA
CBHW071503080526
44587CB00014B/2195